8th AIR FORCE
American heavy bomber groups in England, 1942-1945

Gregory Pons

(Computer graphics by Nicolas Gohin)

Histoire & Collections

FOREWORD

The photographs and documents reproduced in this work are all from the author's collection. Every photo album or scrapbook featured here constitutes a unique piece and illustrates the daily life of American airmen assigned to heavy bomber units in England. The average length of their tour of operations was 6 months, and many of them were homesick. Mail was their principal psychological support, and censorship somewhat reduced the feelings they expressed in letter homes to bland statements. Leisure was seldom to be found on the base, but many airmen used their free time preparing photo albums as mementoes of their service. Some had their own cameras, but many servicemen obtained official pictures taken by the unit's own photographers. These shots were duplicated by the unit photo lab and circulated to be pasted in albums or mailed home. These, and other pictures taken in flight or during their stay in England are today a precious testimony.

Until the Normandy invasion on June 6 1944, Allied bombers had been the only means to bring the fire of war into enemy ranks. Their almost daily actions, in daylight for the USAAF, at night by the Royal Air Force, sustained a war front in the West. The limited accuracy of these thousands of raids was offset by hundreds of thousands of civilian casualties, of which a good number worked, voluntarily or under restraint, in the German armament industry. Nevertheless, it is certain that the daylight bombing offensive waged by the American Air Forces, while costly in men and machines, was a permanent threat for Germany and allowed for some relief on the Eastern front.

The Luftwaffe, constantly provoked into battle, was literally worn threadbare. The hard-won Allied air supremacy was therefore a major factor in final victory in Europe. Even if actual German aircraft production was not weakened by the bombing raids, the dearth of trained pilots, the harassment of the transportation network and the utter destruction of fuel plants brought the Nazis to their knees.

Let us look at the faces of these men, we owe them our freedom.

This book is dedicated to the memory of the 47.000 airmen of the 8th Air Force who gave their lives in the prosecution of the air war in the European Theater of Operations.

Gregory Pons

For Charlotte and Martin

TABLE OF CONTENTS

INTRODUCTION

At the end of the 30's, specialists of aerial warfare believed that heavily-armed bombers would be able to penetrate enemy airspace, to avoid defenses and destroy industrial installations, driving the opponent to surrender.

The Eighth Air Force was activated in Savannah, Georgia in February 1942 and was first commanded by general Ira Eaker. The 8th became part of the buildup of US forces in England to invade the Continent, but more than a mighty air force, the 8th AF became the largest aerial organization in History.

Boeing and Consolidated had developed two revolutionary four-engined heavy bombers: the B-17 'Flying Fortress' and the B-24 'Liberator' according to military specifications. These heavily-armed bombers became the tools of the United States Army Air Forces to pursue their strategy of daylight and high-altitude precision bombing.

In 1942 the Royal Air Force had given up daylight bombing because of heavy losses and while the British Bomber Command now flew at night, Americans decided that the USAAF bombardment groups would raid by day.

The Airforce strategists wanted to prove that heavy bomber formations could succeed in hitting German installations and destroying enemy fighters. They were convinced that the war could be won from the air. They were partly right, but the price to pay was high.

1942

In February 1942, a USAAF Headquarters was established in England, at High Wycombe not far away from London.

The first 8th AF bomber landed in England on 1st July 1942. The first bombing operation of the 8th AF took place on 4 July 1942 (Independence Day) when American crews flew six RAF Boston medium bombers over various targets in Holland. During this mission, Major Charles Kegelman succeeded in bringing home his badly damaged plane, and became the first member of the 8th AF to receive the Distinguished Service Cross. The first 8th AF raid with its own planes occurred on 17 August 1942 when twelve B-17s of the 97th Bomb Group attacked the Rouen-Sotteville rail yards in North-western France.

Until the end of that year, the 8th AF was too weak to make any significant impact but it continued to build up its resources. In the fall of 1942, the campaign against the U-boats began with long-range missions to the French Atlantic coast. Such submarine bases as Lorient, Saint-Nazaire and La Pallice were hit.

In December 1942, General Henry H. Arnold, the Air Forces commanding general, set up a committee of operation analysts to prepare a list of potential targets which, if stricken, would hasten the end of the war in Europe. The destruction of

Above.
**This B-17E named 'Yankee Doodle' was part
of a 12- bomber force during the first raid
of the 8th AF on 17 August 1942 when they attacked
the Rouen-Sotteville rail yards in France.**
(Fox news)

these sites would have a far reaching effect on all German aircraft, vehicle and ship production. Ball-bearing plants, an essential asset in aircraft manufacturing, were soon given the same priority as submarine bases.

1943

The South-east of England was covered with American airfields. The island itself turned into a sort of aircraft carrier which became the home of numerous heavy bombardment units. These belonged to three air divisions: the 1st, 2nd and 3rd Air Divisions, whose planes could be identified by a triangle, circle or a square, respectively, painted on the tail and within which an initial identified the Bomb. Group. Each division was divided in Wings, which were divided in groups divided in squadrons.

The three 8th AF air divisions also had their own fighter wings used for escorting bombers and repel enemy fighters.

The anti-submarine campaign continued until the summer of 1943. It was however estimated after the war that two-thirds of all USAAF bombs from January to June 1943 were dropped on submarine bases and did no damage.

The combined bomber offensive of the RAF and USAAF started officially in June 1943 with the issue of Directive 'Poinblank.' The 8th AF was geared to destroy German aircraft and associated industries and attack airfields in Western Europe to neutralize the Luftwaffe.

Targets were switched to the aircraft, ball bearing and oil production centers. Long-range strikes occurred during the summer against aircraft factories. In July 1943 an airman's tour of operations amounted to 25 missions before rotation home. It was calculated that a crew member had a 50/50 chance of surviving that long.

Schweinfurt and Regensburg

The most important raid of the year took place on 17 August 1943, when heavy bomber formations of the 8th AF attacked the ball-bearing factories in Schweinfurt and the Messerschmitt aircraft plant in Regensburg. The 1st and 3rd Divisions despatched 376 B-17s, 315 reached the target area. Plane formations faced almost continuous opposition on the way in. As Regensburg is located very deep in Southern Germany, and as the Germans thought the area was out of the bombers' range, it was decided for the first time that the 3rd Division would raid Regensburg and then fly south over the Alps to North Africa, which was closer from England. This was the beginning of the 'Shuttle' missions. But because of bad weather, the bombers could not fly back to England and had to remain several days in North Africa.

During this raid 60 bombers (36 for the 1st Division and 24 for the 3rd Division) were lost, which represents 16% of the total committed. On 24th August, the 3rd Division shuttling back from Africa bombed the Focke-Wulf plant in Bordeaux along the way.

Schweinfurt was attacked again on 14 October 1943 with 320 planes, 229 actually dropped their bombs and 60 B-17s were lost. Just over the Dutch border their fighter escort turned back at maximum range and 300 Luftwaffe fighters attacked, resulting in these 23% losses.

Such losses were unsustainable and deep penetration raids were halted. However enemy fight-er production had been cut in half. It is possible to see from today's perspective that the Luftwaffe was now declining in numbers and quality whilst the vast fully mobilized and unscathed American plants were turning out B-17s and B-24s by the hundreds.

In the autumn of 1943 radar 'blind' aiming devices were introduced to allow bombing through the cloud cover, while suitable long-range fighters provided a better protection and challenged the Luftwaffe. The USAAF staff knew that the bombers needed a permanent fighter escort and every effort was made to increase its range. External drop tanks were fitted to P-47s and late in 1943 the P-38s and P-51s with drop tanks were delivered in numbers. These planes could fly to Berlin and back.

On 3 November 1943 the 8th AF attacked the port of Wilhelmshaven. It was its first 500-bomber raid and the first time the H2X radar was used by Pathfinder planes for bombing despite overcast. On 13 December 649 bombers raided Bremen, Hamburg and Kiel, and 670 were committed over the Pas-de-Calais (France) on 24 December.

During all of 1943, losses in heavy bomber units remained high as enemy defenses had been reinforced. The Luftwaffe was also constantly coming up with new tactics to wreck the bomber formations, such as the high speed head-on pass. Thus, German pilots had only a few seconds to aim and fire at heavy bombers but were less exposed to their machine guns. Still, evading the bursts from compact 'boxes' of bombers firing together in all directions became an exploit. But aggressive German pilots succeeded in downing too many four-engined bombers. Furthermore, while by mid-1942, 38% of the German fighter strength was on the Western front, this rose to 45% in the spring of 1943.

The Eastern front figures for the same period fell from 43% to only 27%. The US daylight bombing campaign appeared to be one of the most important means for relieving pressure on the Soviet armies.

battered and never recovered from such important losses. Two days later, on 8th March, the heavies of 8th AF were again over Berlin where they lost 37 planes. Berlin became the most fearsome target for any crew member. Each time the name of this city was pronounced at the beginning of the briefing, fear could be read on most faces.

Flak barrages were so thick that it took real luck to fly through them unscathed. And bombers could not alter course and altitude all the time. They needed to fly closely at the same altitude to ensure accurate bomb release. They had no choice, they had to fly through the barrages. And when there was no Flak, fighters could be expected. Hence surviving a mission to Berlin was always a performance.

On 6 July 1944 the King and Queen with 18-year-old Princess Elizabeth escorted by General Doolittle visited several 8thAF stations. At Thurleigh (the 306th BG base) the princess christened a B-17 which had been named 'Rose of York' (serial No 42-102547) in her honor. She is here discussing with Captain Perry Raster's crew and General Doolittle. The 'Rose of York' was lost on 3 February 1945 with another crew on board as she was coming back from a mission to Berlin. No crew member survived.
(USAAF)

1944

During the winter of 1943-44 the V-weapon sites being constructed in the French coastal regions became operational and constituted additional prime targets. A strong effort was directed against such sites to suppress the new threat to England.

The number of missions to complete a tour of operations was raised from 25 to 30; thus increasing by 20% the availability of crews.

The impressive output of the American industry and the dedication of the work force brought an ever greater increase in the number of new military aircraft.

On 6 January 1944, command of the 8th AF was given to General James H. Doolittle. In early spring of 1944, the number of 8th AF heavy bombers was almost 2,000 (40 groups). Then, the bombing effort was switched against the enemy airforce itself.

The 15th Air Force was established in Italy to attack Germany from the South. The United States Strategic Air Forces in Europe (USSTAF) were created to oversee the 8th and 15th AF. USSTAF's aim was to utterly destroy the Luftwaffe as a preliminary to operation 'Overlord,' the Allied landings in Normandy.

This new set-up allowed co-ordination of American airpower over the whole European theater of war.

The 'Big Week' and Berlin

The neutralization of the German fighter force was achieved through a concentrated series of attacks against aviation plants during February and March 1944. USSTAF's first major move was the 'Big Week' from 19 to 25 February 1944, when the 8th and 15th AF combined attacks on aircraft factories.

The long range fighter escorts no longer stuck with the bombers but were allowed to strafe air-

fields and attack any target of opportunity. The Luftwaffe suffered huge losses (in February: 33% of available aircraft). From February to May a total of 2,000 Luftwaffe pilots became casualties. During this same period the USSTAF also suffered heavy losses, but these could be replaced.

On 6 March 1944, the first massive raids occurred over Berlin. 730 heavy bombers were despatched, of which 672 reached the target. This would become the most important air battle of History. The bomber stream, from England to the objective, was severely hit by German fighters. All Luftwaffe assets had been deployed to fight against the heavy bombers. The heart of the Reich was threatened and had to be protected whatever the cost.

The 8th AF lost 69 heavy bombers (the highest figure of the whole war) but the Luftwaffe was

In mid March 1944 the 8th AF and RAF bombers also attacked every airfield within 350 miles of the invasion zone, wrecking them in the last weeks before D-Day.

The Luftwaffe had pulled back its fighters to defend Germany, and when it attempted to redeploy after the invasion this was almost impossible and too late. The Allied supremacy in the air was nearly total, but on 11 April 1944, the 8th AF lost 64 heavy bombers.

After the elimination of the German fighter arm in May 1944, the first missions were flown against oil plants. This campaign continued until March 1945.

These raids quickly made oil products a critical item for the German forces. The position was so serious that enemy operations were often limited by lack of fuels.

8TH AIR FORCE HEAVY BOMB GROUPS ORDER OF BATTLE, MAY 1945

1st AIR DIVISION

1st Wing		40th Wing		41st Wing		94th Wing	
91st BG	[A]	**92d BG**	[B]	**303d BG**	[C]	**351st BG**	[J]
322d BS	LG	325th BS	NV	358th BS	VK	508th BS	YB
323d BS	OR	326th BS	JW	359th BS	BN	509th BS	RQ
324th BS	DF	327th BS	UX	360th BS	PU	510th BS	TU
401st BS	LL	407th BS	PY	427th BS	GN	511th BS	DS
381st BG	[L]	**305th BG**	[G]	**379th BG**	[K]	**401st BG**	[S]
532d BS	VE	364th BS	WF	524th BS	WA	612th BS	SC
533d BS	VP	365th BS	XK	525th BS	FR	613th BS	IN
534th BS	GD	366th BS	KY	526th BS	LF	614th BS	IW
535th BS	MS	422d BS	JJ	527th BS	FO	615th BS	IY
398th BG	[W]	**306th BG**	[H]	**384th BG**	[P]	**457th BG**	[U]
600th BS	N8	367th BS	GY	544th BS	SU	544th BS	-
601st BS	30	368th BS	BO	545th BS	JD	545th BS	-
602d BS	K8	369th BS	W	546th BS	BK	546th BS	-
603d BS	N7	423d BS	RD	547th BS	SO	547th BS	-

Secret units / Leaflet dropping / Electronic warfare

406th BS	J6	36th BS	R4
		422d BS	JJ

Pathfinder units (radar-equipped B-17s & B-24s)

482d BG	-
812th BS	MI
813th BS	PC
814th BS	SI

Groups disbanded or transferred before May 1945

489th BG	[W]	492d BG	[U]
844th BS	4R	856th BS	5Z
845th BS	T4	857th BS	9H
846th BS	8R	858th BS	9A
847th BS	S4	859th BS	X4

3rd AIR DIVISION

13th Wing		45th Wing		4th Wing		93rd Wing	
95th BG	[B]	**96th BG**	[C]	**94th BG**	[A]	**34th BG**	[S]
334th BS	BG	337th BS	QJ	331st BS	QE	4th BS	Q6
335th BS	OE	338th BS	BX	332d BS	XM	7th BS	R2
336th BS	ET	339th BS	AW	333d BS	TS	18th BS	8I
412th BS	QW	413th BS	MZ	410th BS	GL	391st BS	3L
100th BG	[D]	**388th BG**	[H]	**447th BG**	[K]	**385th BG**	[G]
349th BS	XR	560th BS	-	708th BS	CQ	548th BS	GX
350th BS	LN	561st BS	-	709th BS	IE	549th BS	XA
351st BS	EP	562d BS	-	710th BS	IJ	550th BS	SG
418th BS	LD	563d BS	-	711th BS	IR	551st BS	HR
390th BG	[J]	**452d BG**	[L]	**486th BG**	[W]	**490th BG**	[T]
568th BS	BI	728th BS	9Z	832d BS	3R	848th BS	7W
569th BS	CC	729th BS	M3	833d BS	4N	849th BS	W8
570th BS	DI	730th BS	6K	834th BS	2S	850th BS	7Q
571st BS	FC	731st BS	7D	835th BS	H8	851st BS	S3
				487th BG	[P]	**493d BG**	[X]
				836th BS	2G	860th BS	NG
				837th BS	4F	861st BS	G6
				838th BS	2C	862d BS	8M
				839th BS	R5	863d BS	Q4

Weather & photo reconnaissance group

25th BG	-
652d BS	YN
653d BS	WX
654th BS	XN

2nd AIR DIVISION

2d Wing		14th Wing		20th Wing		96th Wing	
389th BG	[C]	**44th BG**	[A]	**93d BG**	[B]	**458th BG**	[K]
564th BS	YO	66th BS	QK	328th BS	GO	752d BS	7V
565th BS	EE	67h BS	NB	329th BS	RE	753d BS	J4
566th BS	RR	68th BS	WQ	330th BS	AG	754th BS	Z5
567th BS	HP	506th BS	GJ	409th BS	YM	755th BS	J3
445th BG	[F]	**392d BG**	[D]	**446th BG**	[H]	**466th BG**	[L]
700th BS	IS	576th BS	CI	704h BS	FL	784th BS	T9
701st BS	MK	577th BS	DC	705th BS	HN	785th BS	2U
702d BS	WV	578th BS	EC	706th BS	RT	786th BS	U8
703d BS	RN	579th BS	GC	707th BS	JU	787th BS	6L
453d BG	[J]	**491st BG**	[Z]	**448th BG**	[I]	**467th BG**	[P]
732d BS	E3	852d BS	3Q	712th BS	CT	788th BS	X7
733d BS	F8	853d BS	T8	713th BS	IG	7895th BS	6A
734th BS	E8	854th BS	6X	714th BS	EI	790th BS	Q2
735th BS	H6	855th BS	V2	715th BS	IO	791st BS	4Z

Caption

Bombardment group	Tail/wing ID marking
Bombardment squadron	Fuselage marking

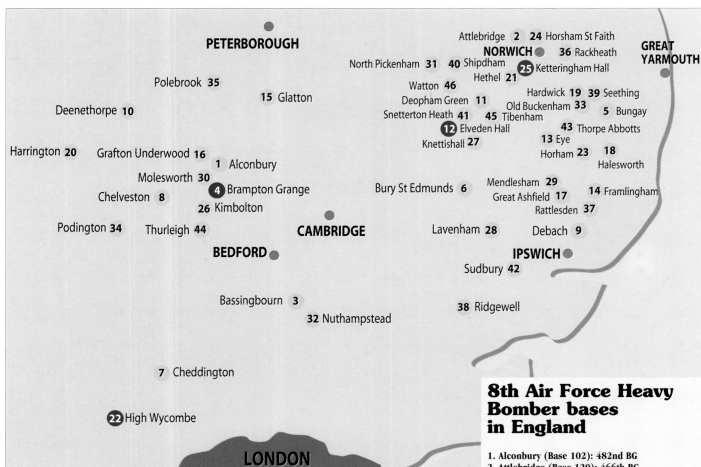

PETERBOROUGH

Polebrook **35**

Deenethorpe **10**

15 Glatton

Harrington **20** Grafton Underwood **16**
1 Alconbury

Molesworth **30**
4 Brampton Grange

Chelveston **8**
26 Kimbolton

Podington **34** Thurleigh **44**

BEDFORD

CAMBRIDGE

Attlebridge **2** **24** Horsham St Faith
NORWICH **36** Rackheath
North Pickenham **31** **40** Shipdham
25 Ketteringham Hall
Hethel **21**
Watton **46**
Deopham Green **11** Hardwick **19** **39** Seething
Snetterton Heath **41** **45** Old Buckenham **33**
5 Bungay
12 Elveden Hall Tibenham
Knettishall **27** **43** Thorpe Abbotts
13 Eye
Horham **23** **18**
Halesworth

Bury St Edmunds **6** Mendlesham **29**
Great Ashfield **17** **14** Framlingham
Rattlesden **37**

Lavenham **28** Debach **9**

IPSWICH

Sudbury **42**

GREAT YARMOUTH

Bassingbourn **3**

32 Nuthampstead

38 Ridgewell

7 Cheddington

22 High Wycombe

LONDON

D-Day

In June 1944 the Americans had 1.200 more bombers and 1.000 more fighters than in January. On 6 June 1944, D-Day began with 3 airborne divisions of 24.000 men dropped beyond the beachheads. Bombers dropped 10.000 tons of bombs on coastal defenses just before landing craft hit the beaches. The 8th and 9th AF had 3.000 planes in the air.

The aerial bombardment prevented any significant counterattack, surprise was total. Released from tactical operations in support of the ground forces, the 8th AF flew a number of missions against German military vehicle factories during the late summer of 1944. These vehicles would have been very useful during the retreat from France.

But by mid June 1944 the V1 rockets started to be launched against London from northern France and both American and British bombers were committed in a considerable effort to destroy their launching sites.

During the fall, important losses were again suffered by the 8th AF heavy bombardment groups. The new German jet fighters were pitted against bomber formations: on 11th September 40 bombers were lost during massive raids on synthetic oil plants and refineries. 35 bombers were also lost 2 days after on 12th September due to a strong fighter force. On 28th september 34 heavy bombers were lost once more due to enemy fighters.

The Luftwaffe was still efficient even if the lack of pilots started to become a real problem. There were still planes but experienced pilots could not be turned out as fast. On 7 October, 40 bombers were lost, still during the strategic campaign against oil refineries. 40 more heavy bombers were lost on 2 November 1944 and 34 on 26 November, the price of the victory in the air was indeed high.

On 24 December, the 8th AF succeeded in deploying 2.046 heavy bombers (1.884 effective) escorted by 813 fighters to attack German airfields but USSTAF soon realized that they needed to concentrate more on refineries and fuel plants which are so precious for a modern army.

1945

At the end of 1944, the number of missions to complete a tour of operations passed from 30 to 35. The strategic assault was turned against the German transportation network, on a larger scale than ever.

Roads and railroads was devastated and German industrial production plummeted. During the final weeks of the war the havoc caused by the heavy bombers had a very strong effect upon the German war economy. In February 1945 Allied air power was so important that thousands of tons of bombs were dropped on Berlin and on the 13th, 14th and 15th the fearful firestorm of Dresden resulted in over 35,000 deaths. If heavy civilian casualties might be deplored, they were and are an inevitable part of the greater involvement of a whole nation in a modern war.

Even if the USAAF commanding officers were convinced that precision bombing could save civilian lives, incorrect target identifications and incorrect sightings caused civilian casualties. The use of radar in bombing through overcast also brought an increase in civilian losses.

Final Victory

On 8 May 1945 the war was over in Europe and the air power of the 8th AF was available for relocation to the Pacific against Japan. With the use of the atomic weapon, the war ended sooner in the Pacific and the Japanese finally surrendered. Most of the 8th AF planes were ferried back from

8th Air Force Heavy Bomber bases in England

1. Alconbury (Base 102): 482nd BG
2. Attlebridge (Base 120): 466th BG
3. Bassingbourn (Base 121): 91st BG
4. Brampton Grange: QG 1st Air Division
5. Bungay (Base 125): 446th BG
6. Bury Saint Edmunds (Base 468): 94th BG
7. Cheddington (Base 113): 406th BS
8. Chelveston (Base 105): 305th BG, 422nd BS
9. Debach (Base 152): 493rd BG
10. Deenethorpe (Base 128): 401st BG
11. Deopham Green (Base 142): 452nd BG
12. Elveden Hall (Base 116): QG 3rd Air Division
13. Eye (Base134): 490th BG
14. Framlingham (Base 153): 390th BG
15. Glatton (Base 130): 457th BG
16. Grafton Underwood (Base 106): 384th BG
17. Great Ashfield (Base 155): 385th BG
18. Halesworth (Base 365): 489th BG
19. Hardwick (Base 104): 93rd BG
20. Harrington (Base 179): 492nd BG
21. Hethel (Base 114): 389th BG
22. High Wycombe: QG 8th Air Force
23. Horham (Base 119): 95th BG
24. Horsham St Faith (Base 123): 458th BG
25. Ketteringham Hall: QG 2nd Air Division
26. Kimbolton (Base 117): 379th BG
27. Knettishall (Base 136): 388th BG
28. Lavenham (Base 137): 487th BG
29. Mendlesham (Base 156): 34th BG
30. Molesworth (Base 107): 303rd BG
31. North Pickenham (Base 143): 491st BG
32. Nuthampstead (Base 131): 398th BG
33. Old Buckenham (Base 144): 453rd BG
34. Podington (Base 109): 92nd BG
35. Polebrook (Base 110): 351st BG
36. Rackheath (Base 145): 467th BG
37. Rattlesden (Base 126): 447th BG
38. Ridgewell (Base 167): 381stBG
39. Seething (Base 146): 453th BG
40. Shipdham (Base 115): 44th BG
41. Snetterton Heath (Base 138): 96th BG
42. Sudbury (Base 174): 486th BG
43. Thorpe Abbots (Base 139): 100th BG
44. Thurleigh (Base 111): 306th BG
45. Tibenham (Base 124): 445th BG
46. Watton (Base 376): 25th BG

Left.
On November 11th 1943 'Knock-Out Dropper' of the 303d BG came back safely to claim first honors for being the first plane in the European theater of operations to complete 50 operational flights. Congratulations are in order from pilot 1st Lt. Malcolm E. Brown, left, to her crew chief, M/Sgt Budford Pafford, at right. Capt. George T Mackin who went on the record making flight as co-pilot, is in the center.
(USAAF)

England to the USA where they were parked in desert areas before being scrapped.

In the European war, strategic bombings played a major part in the downfall of Nazi Germany. The whole 8th AF had 350.000 soldiers; 200.000 were combat crews.

World war II statistics of casualties compared to the total personnel strength were: 1% for the navy; 2% for the Army (as a whole); 3% for the Marines; 7% for the Army Air Forces (as a whole) of which 27% were aircrews!

During the summer of 1943, the crew of the 'Memphis Belle' (91st BG) became one of the first B-17 crews to complete 25 daylight bombing raids over Germany and occupied Europe. Captain Robert K. Morgan, the pilot, and his crew are pictured while the crew chief is painting a 25th bomb on the fuselage for this last mission.
(USAAF)

Inset, top left.
The 306th Bomb. Group insignia

Above.
The early missions. A formation of B-17s heads for its target through the clouds. The combat unit markings have not been painted on yet.

306th Bomb Group

1. 306TH BOMB. GROUP

**367TH BOMB SQUADRON
TECHNICAL SERGEANT
HARRY M. BROWN
RADIO-GUNNER
25 MISSIONS**

The 306th Bomb. Group was one of the pioneer units involved in the European Air War. It was the first to fly into Germany. The group was established on January 28, 1942 with 4 squadrons (367th, 368th, 369th and 423rd BS) and moved to England in August and September 1942. Its first commanding officer was Colonel Charles Overacker, who was replaced by Colonel Frank A. Armstrong Jr on January 3, 1943. The unit was stationed in Thurleigh (Station 111). At the beginning of October 1942, B-17s from the group attacked several types of strategic targets in France. On January 27, 1943, the 306th BG was the first unit to penetrate into Germany to strike the U-boat pens at Wilhemshaven. Sergeant Maynard H. Smith, a gunner, was awarded the Medal of Honor for his action during a mission on May 1, 1943. His aircraft was hit by the enemy and fires started in the fuselage. Maynard manned his machine gun until the German fighters gave up their chase. Then he administered first aid to the wounded tail gunner and suc-ceeded in extinguishing the fire.

On January 11th, the 306th BG and several other bomb. groups of the 8th Air Force took part in an important raid against aircraft factories in Central Germany. For its action on this day the 306th was awarded a first Distinctive Unit Citation (DUC). Soon after, it was awarded a second DUC for its participation in the 'Big Week:' the intensive aerial campaign against the German aircraft industry, from February 20th to 25th 1944. In preparation of the

(Continued on page 10)

Brown's crew posing near a B-17. Note the early pattern of American star on the fuselage.

DIARY OF THE CLAY PIGEON SQUADRON
BY HARRY MILTON BROWN

"The air had just been washed clean by a heavy rainfall as we descended from the sub-stratosphere. Lt. Buckey downed quietly our B-17 on the rain-washed runway at Prestwick airdrome, and in my estimation we had won our first big battle by crossing the Atlantic Ocean.

You could see the fresh sun rays eating up the water puddles as we taxied to our dispersal area, and I felt greatly at ease. As radio operator, I secured my radio transmitter and checked my Hershey bars. It was combat I wanted, so here I was part of a well-trained bomber crew of the Eighth Air Force.

This was the 2nd of September 1942 and in little more than one month we were making our first raid on enemy territory. October 9, 1942, orders came thru to attack Lille. It was very successful!

All planes from the four squadrons of the 306th Bomb Group returned safely.

Weather proved rather poor for bombing missions for the rest of the month, although there were many alerts and briefings. November 7, 8 and 9th, we attacked the sub pens of Brest, La Pallice and Saint-Nazaire respectively. Submarines were causing great havoc on the high seas and our first and prime job was to knock out the home bases of these deadly raiders.

Further raids against Lorient, Saint-Nazaire and Romilly-sur-Seine in November and December were proving rather costly.

With no fighter protection in our favor and encountering heavy Flak areas it was showing its toll. A total of twenty five missions was our goal; as then you were replaced and returned to glory and the U.S.

It was January 9th and twenty five missions looked a long long way off! The 306th had lost a total of 15 planes and out of our four squadrons, the 367th squadron was really hit the hardest. We had lost a total of 8 ships with a contingent of 14 officers and enlisted men. It sure was a different feeling than our first mission revealed.

Our barracks that was always a gay land and noisy home was silenced, and empty bunks devoted those we lost. New crews came in to replace the ones lost... but it was pitiful. Our 367th squadron really seems to be taking it right in the pants. Course we old timers were always hoping a change was to come.

It was the 15th of January when word came that the officials were going to take our ship #64 away from us. Our Fortress didn't have a name smeared on her sides, but we fellows called her 'Raunchy.' There was only one other ship #64 called 'The Lone Ranger' that was left from the original group to cross the ocean together.

She was returning from a raid on the coast and went down as fog settled in either by loss of gas or fighters.

I hated to see them take our ship from us as that ship took us across the ocean and through many a tough daylight raid over German held territory. It had so many patches on it... it looked like a damn quilt.

January 20, we received our new ship! Number 306 is the number on the tail: same as the group! It has the new demand oxygen system and a good radio I hope... which will all be checked out. Most important, we were assigned two new men: Sgt. Emil Miller and the other Sgt. Eugen Kennedy from the state of New York.

January 27 was a big day. It was just another raid to me but Generals, Colonels, War Correspondents and many notables were awaiting our return. It was to go down in History as the first daylight raid on Germany!

I was at my radio gun position ans it was quite a difference from my first raid when attacked by

Above, right.
The 367th Bomb. Squadron insignia.

Above.
Harry Brown is perched atop the fuselage of a B-17, just over his station as radio operator/gunner. The GY marking was the identification code for the 367th Bomb. Squadron.

Right.
Harry Brown's portrait before leaving the USA. Brown started his service as a gunner/radio operator, to be later commissioned as an armament officer in three bombardment groups.

Bottom.
In this early studio portrait, Brown wields his .45 Caliber pistol.

Below.
Aircrew member wings worn by radio operator/gunners.

"flak enclosed obtained from ship 306 25 that was really hit with "flak"!

enemy fighters. The radio room was so full of spent cartridges it was impossible to walk.

Bad weather held up operations for some time and all we could do was some ground training and passes to London.

It was the 1st of March that we returned from London and went into our quarters expecting to get the big Hello. There was a blank reception. Our hut was empty and a dismal spell seemed to be cast over it. Barracks bags were all packed, foot lockers and flight bags were packed, shelves were all cleaned.

Girlfriend pictures and favorite family pictures disappeared. We couldn't imagine what had happened. We ran over to the other huts of our fellow squadron members. More bags packed, more shelves cleaned. Foot lockers closed and locked. It started to be sickening! We fastened over to the last combat hut. One lonely man, grounded because of illness was playing a lonesome game of solitaire. We asked him what this all means. Afraid to listen, he told us the loss of Capt. Ryan, his entire crew, together with Lt. Turmell and his full crew. This was the last of our original friends and the birth of the 'Clay Pigeon Squadron.'

But War is Hell and operations had us up the very next day. Our squadron had been depleted so we filled in with another squadron. Our target was the Nazis airfields and plane factories. We had orders to knock out the Ford and GMC plants in Antwerp.

Fock Wulfs and Me 109s were thicker than gums underneath movie seats. Flak charges plus aerial bombs also caused their damage to our group.

We were flying left wing in the low element of group leading the attack. Being the first group over the target we caught Royal Hell. Head-on attacks by FWs really got us. Our ship was being cut to ribbons with 20-mm shells and smaller caliber all over it. It sure looked like we were going to join former buddies... but our exceptional pilot George Buckey kept a tight formation that gave excellent fire power.

The second element of our squadron didn't fare well at all as Jerry fighters knocked them out completely. German fighters were buzzing around us like bees around honey. Thank God we managed to limp back safely to base..."

B-17s of the 306th BG flying through a Flak barrage, the black puffs are caused by anti aircraft shells. The target area seems to be shrouded in clouds.

Inset.
This small piece of metal is a Flak shell fragment picked up by sergeant Brown after it had hit his B-17.

Below.
Two officers waiting for the return of the planes after a mission.

Normandy invasion, the group struck airfields and marshalling yards in France and Belgium. On June 6th, its B-17s bombed railroads and coastal batteries and during the whole Normandy campaign, the group supported ground troops.

On September 16th, its planes flew to help with airborne operations in Holland. From December 1944 to March 1945, the 306th BG was involved in the destruction of marshalling yards and airfields during the Battle of the Bulge, in the crossing of the Rhine supporting the airborne assault and in the systematic destruction of transport and communications networks.

After V-E day, the 306th BG remained in Europe. It was then committed to a special photographic and mapping program from Western Europe to North Africa. It was inactivated in Germany on December 25, 1946. From October 1942 to April 1945, in 342 combat missions, the 306th BG lost 171 B-17s in action.

SECRET.

306 B.G.   (1.BW/102.BGBW.)

BOMBER COMMAND
COMBAT REPORT.

Date .... (A)

Squadron No. .... (B)   As R.of Ldr Box 1.

Number of Enemy Aircraft .... (C)

Type of Enemy Aircraft .... (D)

Time Attack was delivered .... (E)

Place Attack was delivered .... (F)

Height of Enemy .... (G)

Enemy Casualties .... (H)

Our Casualties .... Aircraft .... (J)

GENERAL REPORT .... War Mission STUTTGART
T/O Thurleigh   09.50 hrs.

Combat commenced after e/a attacked at 26 ,000 ft near target.
Gunners drew fire from 500 yds closing to 200. Fuselage racked
wounding W/G. Enemy rolled U/A and B/gunner opened up with T.

E/fighter hit and smoke noted from port side of engine. Enemy
seen to break for cloud and nothing more seen of him.

B17 seen to go down to S/B from e/A attack .Number possibly 48572.

Ship damaged cat 4. but RTB okay. S/Sgt Barry G/S wound to left
chest. U/c on landing and further condition U/K at this point.

File report for enquiry.

                                        F 6 SEP 1943

                        Signature   GRP. INT. OFF.

                        Squadron No.

Harry Brown Is Decorated

Sgt. Brown

Sgt. Harry Milton Brown, son of Mr. and Mrs. Simon Brown, 625 Front street, Brownsville, was one of four area men recently awarded air medals for their part in recent air raids on the submarine base at Lorient in German-held France.

Sgt. Brown is a radio-gunner on an American Flying Fortress and has been stationed in England for some months. He was the first Brownsville boy to make a trans-Atlantic flight, flying to England from this country.

Others in the district among 20 Pennsylvanians awarded air medals for participation in bombing attacks were: Michael Roskovich, gunner, Fayette City, R. D. 1; Ervin Grenke, engineer, Fairhope, R. D. 1 and Capt. James E. O'Brien, pilot, Monongahela, R. D. 1.

Top, left.
This 'secret' combat report covers the 306th BG mission over Stuttgart on September 3, 1943. A B-17 badly damaged is reported going down after being hit by enemy fighters.

Top, right.
Singer Trishie Howard, Hollywood actor Leslie Howard's ('Gone with the wind') daughter-in-law, finds in Harry Brown a partner and fan who knows all her tunes.

Left.
Soon after his arrival in Great Britain, Harry Brown poses in the traditional Highland garb for this studio shot.

Right.
This newspaper cutting mentions that Brown was awarded the Air Medal for his participation in air raids against German submarines bases in France.

351st BOMB. GROUP

509TH BOMB SQUADRON
2D LIEUTENANT HARRY M. BROWN
GUNNERY OFFICER

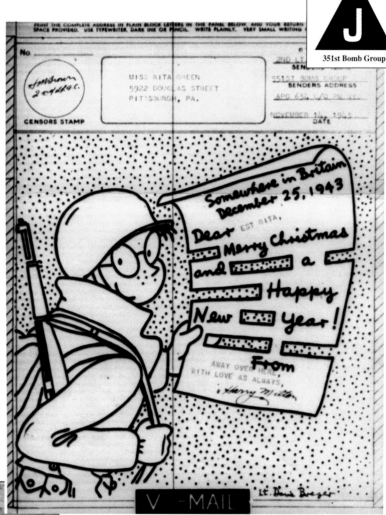

Top, right.
The 509th Bomb. Squadron Insignia.

Above.
**This V-mail was just
sent before Christmas by Brown.**

Right.
**This V-mail (Victory Mail) letter was sent by Harry Brown to his fiancée who
lived in Pittsburgh as the end of the 1943 was near. Brown had been transferred
to the 351st BG a short time before.**

Harry Brown, who had been commissioned as a 2nd Lieutenant while with
the 306th BG was transferred in August 1943 to the 351st BG as Armament
Officer. He is pictured with other officers of his new unit. Note the 509th BS
patch on his tanker's jacket.

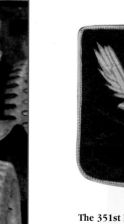

The 351st Bomb. Group insignia.

305TH BOMB. GROUP

442D BOMB SQUADRON
2D LIEUTENANT HARRY M. BROWN
GUNNERY OFFICER

After leaving the 351st BG, Brown was assigned briefly to the 384th Bomb. Group between May and July 1944. He was then transferred again, this time to the 305th BG and remained with this unit as armament officer until the end of the war.

305th Bomb Group

Above.
A B-17F of the 305th BG was pictured during a mission over Germany. Note the smoke screens on the ground, laid to cover the target area and make bomb sighting more difficult.
(USAAF)

Left.
Lieutenant Brown's pay data card. He still drew additional 'flying' pay even though filling a ground assignment.

Below.
The 305th BG base at Chelveston. The ambulances were made ready near the runway as first planes of the group were approaching the airdrome.
(USAAF)

The 305th Bomb. Group insignia.

OFFICER'S PAY DATA CARD

LAST NAME – FIRST NAME – MIDDLE INITIAL				ARMY SERIAL NUMBER	
BROWN, Harry M.				02044608	
GRADE	ARM OR SERVICE	PAY PER 100	LENGTH OF SERV.	DATE YEARS COMPLETED	
1stLt	AC	2	OVER 3 YEARS	4 Nov '44	
PAY AND ALLOWANCES				AMOUNT	
MONTHLY BASE PAY AND LONGEVITY				175	00
ADDITIONAL PAY FOR Flying				87	50
ADDITIONAL PAY FOR					
SUBSISTENCE (30 DAY MONTH)				42	00
RENTAL ALLOWANCE				75	00
			TOTAL	379	50
30 Jul '45 ALLOTMENTS, DEDUCTIONS AND STOPPAGES					
CLASS E				200 00	200 00
INSURANCE		D	N	6.60	6 60
CLASS B					
OTHER DEDUCTIONS (SPECIFY)					
SUBSEQUENT CHANGES IN ABOVE DATA WITH DATES			TOTAL	206	60
			NET	172	90
DEPENDENTS (STATE NAMES AND ADDRESSES)					
Rita G. Brown(wife)					

WD AGO FORM 77 11 FEBRUARY 1943
THIS FORM SUPERSEDES W.D., A.G.O. FORM NO. 77, 29 JUNE 1944 WHICH WILL NOT BE USED AFTER RECEIPT OF THIS REVISION.

Below.
A chart of the Bremen area serves as backdrop for this composition:
- **Calendar pages graced with pin-up girls**
- **8th Air Force technical bulletins for air crews**
- **Period cigarette packs and matchbooks**
- **Decks of playing cards**
- ***Life* magazine of July 23, 1943 with a photo-feature on bombers based in Britain**
- **Manual for aircraft gunners**
- **A leather Navigator's case, an E-6B plastic computer, an A-8 issue chronograph, an A-11 aviator's wristwatch, a load ajuster and its leather case.**

Planes of the 305th BG are dropping their bombs on the fringe of the cloud cover which, just few minutes later, would completely shroud the target. This prohibited accurate bomb-sighting, and bombardiers would then resort to bomb 'blind' using radar.
(USAAF)

14

NAVIGATOR, MAY 1943

May 19, 1943. 306th Bomb. Group crews are about to take off for a mission over Kiel harbor in Germany. 22 B-17-Fs will be committed on this long flight. The objective is bound to be strongly defended by Flak, thick cloud cover is forecast and will hinder accurate aiming but, what's most, the Luftwaffe fighter arm is expected to put up a vigorous fight to defend the Kriegsmarine ships.

This navigator will soon take his seat at the chart table, aft the bombardier's position in the nose. His flying gear is made up of the following:
- B-6 flying helmet with leather cups for the earphones
- Mk VIII Royal Air Force goggles
- T-30 throat microphone
- A-9 gloves
- A-4 summer flying suit
- F-1 electrically-heated suit. Its lead and plug are visible near our man's right hand
- A-2 leather flight jacket
- B-3 life preserver
- Pattern 1940 RAF flying boots
- Back-type B-7 parachute and harness. The wide chest strap has been slipped under the life preserver so as not to impede its inflating
- H-1 emergency bail-out oxygen bottle (in a boot shaft)

This Airforce officer also has a navigator's leather case for charts and various instruments. He might be considered as the crew's most important part, the one that will lead them straight to the target and then safely home…

(Reconstruction, photo Militaria Magazine)

The B-7 back-type parachute.

AN EIGHTH AIR FORCE BOM-
BER STATION, ENGLAND: The
phrase, "It's a small world," cer-
tainly applies to the meeting of
First Lieutenants Harry M. Brown
and Andrew L. Dudzak, both of
Brownsville, Pa., and gunnery officers with the 305th Bombardment Group.

They climbed into a B-17 Flying Fortress for a routine cross-
country flight to another aero-
drome without noticing each other.
Lt. Brown heard that a newly arrived gunnery officer was making
the flight in the waist position.
He called him on the plane's in-
ter-con:

"This is Brown, squadron gunnery officer. I understand you've
just come from the States assigned to the Group as a gunnery officer. If I can do anything for you,
just let me know. By the way,
what's your name?"

"Dudzak."

"Where're you from?"

"Brownsville, Pennsylvania."

"Brownsville?! Why, that's my
hometown! . . . Dudzak . . . Say,
didn't you teach at the high school
there?"

"No, that was my brother—Joe."

"Well, I'll be darned; he taught
me in my junior year!"

The two officers from Brownsville not only share a common
background, but also hold identical
jobs in their respective squadrons.
As gunnery officers they must
train and "check out" new crews
on gunnery, fighter tactics, and
formations, instructing them in the
various gun sights and the value
of defensive and supporting fire.

Lt. Brown, the 25-year-old son
of Mr. and Mrs. Simon Brown, 628
Front street, Brownsville, entered
the AAF in November, 1941, and
came to the European Theater of
Operations on September 2, 1942,
as an enlisted man and radio oper-
ator-gunner on a combat crew.
He completed a tour of operations
during which he was awarded the
Distinguished Flying Cross and
the Air Medal with three Oak
Leaf clusters.

Brown, after his graduation
from Brownsville high school in
1938, and was employed as manager
and buyer of men's clothing by
R. Shure, Market St., Brownsville.

Lt. Dudzak enlisted in the AAF
in November, 1939, and a few years
later was commissioned as a gunnery officer. He arrived in the
European Theater of Operations in
March, 1945. He is the son of Mr.
and Mrs. Joseph A. Dudak, 713
Howard street, Brownsville, where
he graduated from Brownsville
high school with the class of 1935.

Two Brownsville, Pa., officers meet at an Eighth Air Force Station in England, where they are gunnery officers. Left First Lieutenant Harry M. Brown shows First Lieutenant Andrew L. Dudzak part
of a .50 calibre machine gun carried by the B-17 Flying Fortress.

This picture and article were published in a
newspaper about the meeting between Harry
Brown and another officer, both from the same
hometown: Brownsville (Penn.). They were
photographed while inspecting 50 cal. machine
gun barrels. On the left Harry Brown is wearing
many medal ribbons (DFC, Air Medal with oak
leaf clusters, Good Conduct Medal...). Note
the lack of service ribbons on the shirt of the
other officer, newer in the service.
(USAAF)

16

A flight in formation over occupied Europe. Note the impressive mission tally on the nose of the foremost machine.
(USAAF)

Left.
Brown and other 305th BG officers.

Bombs bays are open, B-17s let go of their load. Note the aluminum finish of this B-17G, the thin plumes of the smoke markers on the ground and the reflection of the sun on the cloud cover on the left of the shot.
(USAAF)

Landing at Chelveston. At the beginning of the runway stands a checkered wagon fitted with a plexiglas dome (a B-17 reclaimed part) and a wind socket. Standing inside, a radio operator was in contact with the pilot and was a precious help for ensuring a safe landing after a long and strenuous flight.
(USAAF)

2. 381ST BOMB. GROUP

**533RD BOMB. SQUADRON
1ST LT. RICHARD SCHMIDT
PILOT
30 MISSIONS**

The 381st Bomb. Group was established on October 28, 1942 with four squadrons (532nd, 533rd, 534th and 535th BS). It moved to England between May and June 1943 under the leadership of Colonel Joseph J. Nazzaro and made its home at Ridgewell airbase (base 167). The group began its combat missions in June against various objectives, such as an aircraft factory at Villacoublay near Paris, a German airfield at Amiens, the Saint-Nazaire docks, nitrate mines in Norway and industrial areas near Münster. Until June 1945, the 381st BG took part in all of the 8th AF's strategic bombing flights over Occupied Europe. It was awarded a Distinguished Unit Citation for the accuracy of its bombing over Bremen on October 3, 1943, despite heavy flak and fighter opposition. The group received another citation for its successful participation in raids against aeronautical works in Central Germany on January 11, 1944. The same month, Colonel Harry P. Leber replaced Col. Nazzaro as group CO. Between 20 and 25 February, the unit was involved in the 'Big Week.' It was also committed to the tactical support of ground troops and to striking several types of targets. On June 6, the group's mission was to destroy bridges and airfields adjacent to the Normandy beachhead. In July, the 381st also helped ground troops in the breakout at Saint-Lô. During the Battle of the Bulge, the 381st BG harassed German communications and fighter bases. It then supported the Rhine crossings.

All through March 1945, its aircraft were committed to wrecking the enemy road and transportation network. The

Above.
September 23, 1943, at the Rapid City (South Dakota) airbase. Lieutenant Schmidt's crew is pictured at the conclusion of its training before being assigned to a combat unit in England. Schmidt is standing, top row, 2nd from the left.
(USAAF)

Right.
December 1942, Air cadet Schmidt photographed as a student in flight gear at Morton Air Academy in California. He has the old-style flying helmet with Gosport tubes instead of intercom earphones, as used on some trainer aircraft.

The 381st Bomb. Group insignia.

group was shipped home between June and July 1945, it was inactivated on August 28, 1945.

From June 1943 to April 1945, while flying a total of 296 missions, the 381st BG combat losses were 131 aircraft.

Left.
At Santa Ana, during pre-flight training and personnel classification, members of Squadron 21 are in front of their tent. Schmidt is 2nd from the left.
(RR)

Below.
One of the Vultee Valiant trainers flown by Schmidt at Minter Field, near Bakersfield, California. This plane was nicknamed 'The Vibrator'.
(RR)

Inset, below.
Certificate awarded to Richard Schmidt when he left Morton Air Academy in Blythe, California.

Air Force Training Detachment
Morton Air Academy
Blythe, California
Awards this
Certificate of Completion
To **Richard J. Schmidt**
who has satisfactorily completed sixty hours of flying in Primary Training at Gary Field and has successfully passed written examinations in Navigation, Meteorology, Identification, Aerodynamics, Aircraft, Engines, Propellers and related Chemistry Physics and Mathematics. Due to his cooperation, Citizenship, attitude and industry, he carries with him the unreserved recommendation of this school. Dated this thirty-first day of December, Nineteen Hundred Forty-Two.
President.

AIR FORCES ADVANCED FLYING SCHOOL
ROSWELL ARMY FLYING SCHOOL
ROSWELL, N. M.

Letterhead of the Roswell Airforce flying school.

Above.
Cadet Schmidt in flying suit in front of a Vultee Valiant trainer.

The first mail sent by Schmidt to his parents from California. This was actually a form printed on the base, the boys just had to fill the blanks before mailing it.

SANTA ANA ARMY AIR BASE
SANTA ANA, CALIFORNIA

august 31 , 1942

Dear Mother :

I'm sending this from the Classification Center here at the Santa Ana Army Air Base, where I arrived today. I was met at the train and am now here with the rest of the future Army Air Crews.

I've been registered and assigned to Squadron 21, where I shall remain for about two weeks. During that time I will have my physical examinations and tests which will determine whether I become a Pilot, Bombardier, or Navigator. After being classified, I will be assigned to another squadron here on this post, and then my actual preflight training begins. That preflight training will last for about nine weeks and then I will be sent to one of the flying schools to start my flying training.

You will, no doubt, think it strange receiving this type of letter from me instead of a personal note, but here is why: Our Commanding Officer knows that during the excitement and process of getting settled during the next few days, some of us will be apt to forget to write to the folks at home. This is his way of letting you know where I am and that I am well. It's just one of the many indications that I shall be well taken care of in the Army Air Forces. Another is my protection by National Service Life Insurance which is granted me free of charge all through my training period.

I know I'll have more nice things to tell you when I write a real letter. In the meantime, please let me hear from you. My address is:

Squadron 21
Army Air Base
Santa Ana, Calif.

20   P.S.— The food is wonderful

Love
Dick

Above.
Dated January 22, 1943, this document appointed Cadet Schmidt as a 'Flight sergeant' with certain command prerogatives…

Right.
March 1943. Schmidt and his classmates in Aviation Cadet uniforms. These were similar to commissioned officers' uniforms, except for the collar devices and winged propeller cap insignia.

Left.
May 1943: a rare color photo showing Schmidt's and his roommates at Roswell. From left to right: Geo. Schock, Richard Schmidt and Bob Sherfey. Schmidt still wears his Morton Air Academy undershirt.
(RR)

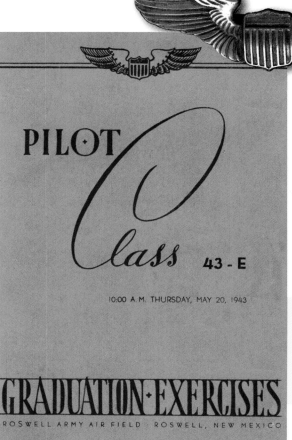

Above.
Pilot wings

Right.
Press article dated March 17, 1943 relating Schmidt's progress in his army career.

Richard J. Schmidt To Get Commission

Aviation Cadet Richard J. Schmidt, 21, son of Mr. and Mrs. E. R. Schmidt of 6346 S. E. Stephens street, has completed basic training at Minter field, Cal., and is now in advanced training at Roswell, N. M. He is scheduled to receive his commission in May.

Schmidt is a graduate of Franklin high school and was associated with the Binyon Optical company here. He attended the North Pacific College of Optometry. Schmidt enlisted in the army air corps in April, 1942, and reported for pre-flight training at Santa Ana, Cal., in July, 1942. He took primary training at Blythe, Cal. During basic training he was made flight sergeant for his unit.

JOURNAL
3/17/43

Occupants of hut #13 near the entrance of a shelter at the 381st BG Ridgewell airfield. From left to right: Bonomo, Schmidt, Wolbrink, Townsend, Helm, Barr. Note the 533rd Bomb Squadron patch on the flying jackets.

Right.
Newspaper cutting of November 24, 1943. Freshly-commissioned Schmidt is ready to leave the USA for an overseas combat posting.

Below.
At Ridgewell airbase: a view of the inside of Schmidt's Nissen hut, which he shared with other officers. From left to right: lieutenants Barr, Townsend and Helm.

JOURNAL 11/24/43

Army Air Lieutenant Comes Home on Leave

Following graduation from the Rapid City, S. D., army air base, 2d Lieut. Richard J. Schmidt, son of Mr. and Mrs. E. R. Schmidt, 6346 SE Stephens street, is home on leave. He has completed various phases of operational flight training.

Entering the army in April, 1942, he trained at Santa Ana, Cal., Blythe, Cal., Minter field, and Roswell, N. M., where he won his wings in May as a bomber pilot. He is a graduate of Franklin high school, attended the North Pacific College of Optometry and was employed for two years by the Binyon Aptical company.

R. J. Schmidt

Schmidt's crew in front of a B-17G. Schmidt is in the
back row, second from the right, wearing sunglasses.
Sitting are Royal Air Force ground crews.
(USAAF)

The 533rd Bomb.
Squadron insignia.

Late in the morning, as the fog is clearing away,
crews are waiting for the signal to start the engines.
(USAAF)

**B-17 G 'Lucky Me' (serial # 42-31570), 381st BG/533rd BS, May 1944.
Lieutenant Schmidt flew his last seven missions, as pilot on this machine. It
was lost on September 25th 1944 during a mission over the Frankfut
marshalling yards with Lt. Oscar Gills's crew.**
(Computer graphics by Nicolas Gohin)

R E S T R I C T E D

General Orders)   Hq Eighth Air Force,
No.   169   )   E X T R A C T   APO 634, 16 March1944.

Under the provisions of Army Regulations 600-45, 22 September 1943, and
pursuant to the authority contained in Restricted Message No. 2139, Hq
USSAFE, 11 January 1944 , the AIR MEDAL is awarded to the following named
Officer.
Citation: For exeptional meritorious achievement, while participating in
five separate bomber combat missions over enemy occupied Continental Europe
The courage, coolness and skill displayed by this Officer upon these occa-
sions reflects great credit upon himself and the Armed Forces of the United
States.Army

*   *   *   *   *   *   *   *

RICHARD J. SCHMIDT, O-746432, 2nd Lieutenant, 533 Bombardment Squadron,
381st Bombardment Group (H), ARMY AIR FORCES, United States Army.
Home address: Portland Oregon.

                    By command of Major General DOOLITTLE.

                                    JOHN A. STAMFORD
                                    Brigadier General, U.S.A.
OFFICIAL: Chief of Staff
EDWARD E. TORO ,
Colonel AGD,
Adjutant General.

Above.
**"Bombs away!" the white plumes are
from the smoke markers dropped
previously to point the target out.**
(USAAF)

Left.
**Dated March 16, 1944, this document
from 8th Air Force HQ awards the Air
Medal to lieutenant Schmidt for having
participated in five combat missions.**

Above.
The Air Medal.

BOEING FLYING
(B-17G)

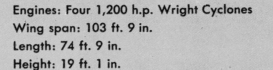

Engines: Four 1,200 h.p. Wright Cyclones
Wing span: 103 ft. 9 in.
Length: 74 ft. 9 in.
Height: 19 ft. 1 in.
Top speed: over 300 m.p.h.

Gross
Servi
Arma
Crew
Wing

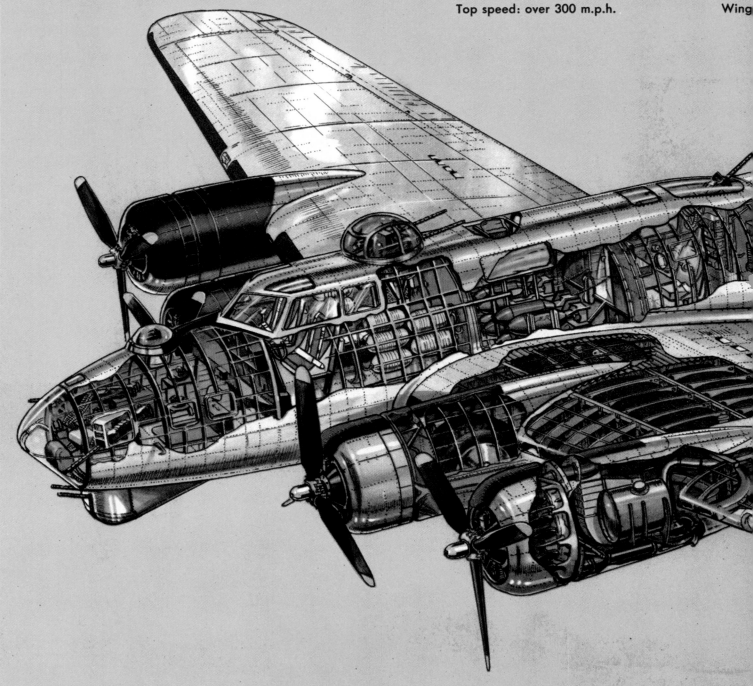

Cut-out view of a B-17G 'Flying Fortress' published in the famous aviation magazine *Flying* during WW2.

RTRESS

65,000 pounds
r 40,000 feet
): 13 guns

lbs. sq. ft.

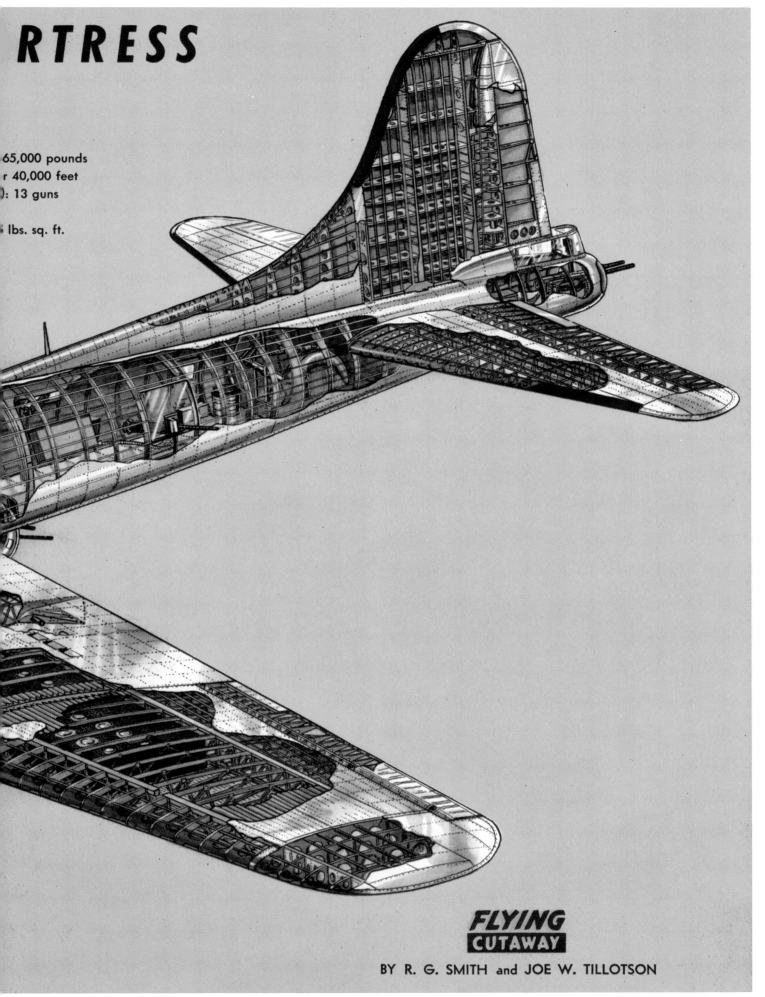

FLYING CUTAWAY

BY R. G. SMITH and JOE W. TILLOTSON

General Orders)
No. 232)   E X T R A C T   Hq Eighth Air Force,
                                                        APO 634, 30 March 1944

    Under the provisions of Army Regulations 600-45, 22 September 1943,
and pursuant to authority contained in Restricted TT Message No. 2139, Hq
USSAFE, 11 January 1944, an OAK LEAF CLUSTER IS AWARDED, for wear with the
Air Medal previously awarded, to the following named Officer, organization
as indicated, Army Air Forces, United States Army.
    CITATION: For exceptionally meritorious achievement, while participat
ing in five separate bomber combat missions over enemy occupied Continental
Europe. The courage, coolness and skill displayed by this Officer upon thes
these occasions reflects great credit upon himself and the Armed Forces of
the United States.
*   *   *   *   *   *   *

                    381st Bombardment Group (H)

RICHARD J. SCHMIDT, O-746432, 2nd Lt. Home address: Portland Oregon,

*   *   *   *   *   *   *

            By comm and of Lieutenant DOOLITTLE:

                                        JOHN A. STAMFORD,
                                        Brigadier General, U.S.A.
                                        Chief of Staff.

OFFICIAL:
EDWARD E. TORO
Colonel, AGD,
Adjutant General.

General Orders No. 302, dated 24 Apr il 1944 awarded the above named
Officer a second OAK-LEAF CLUSTER, for wear with the Air Medal.
*   *   *   *   *   *   *
General Orders No. 329, dated 30 April 1944 awarded the above named
Officer a third OAK LEAF CLUSTER, for wear with the Air Medal.

*   *   *   *   *   *   *

Left.
Dated March 30, 1944, this document added an oak leaf
cluster to lieutenant Schmidt's Air Medal for additional
combat missions. The oak leaf device represents an additional
award of the Air Medal. Two more awards were recorded on
April 24 and 30.

Below.
A 381st BG bomber formation. In foreground, the B-17G
'Lucky Me' coded W*VP (533rd BS, see page 25) was flown by
Lieutenant Schmidt when he became 1st pilot for his last
seven combat missions.
(USAAF)

Opposite page.
Page One of the February 28th 1944 *Stars & Stripes* was
dedicated to 8th AF operations of the previous week. On
Sunday 20 February began operation 'Argument,' forever to be
referred to by its more pungent name of 'Big Week.' In a
single week the 8th AF dropped more bombs than in the first
year of its operation. The main goal was destroying the
German aeronautical industry. During these raids about 2.000
planes were committed. The Germans as a consequence were
compelled to disperse smaller workshops away from large
industrial centers. The February bombings did deny the
enemy serval hundreds of aircraft at a time when they were
badly needed and could probably have been brought into
effective use against the Allied invasion of Europe. But the
effect of the 'Big Week' on German air power was not
restricted to bomb damage. Indeed, there is reason to believe
that the large and fiercely fought air battles of those six
February days had more impact on establishing the air
superiority on which Allied plans depended than did the
bombing of industrial plants.

**1st Lieutenant
Schmidt received
the Distinguished Flying
Cross on May 30, 1944
for extraordinary
achievement while
serving as pilot
of a B-17.**

Left.
**The Distinguished
Flying Cross.**

General Orders)   E X T R A C T   Hqs, Eighth Air
Number 430)   Force,
                                                       APO 634, 30 May 1944

    I. Under the provisions of Army Regulations 600-45, 22 September
1943, as amended, and pursuant to the authority contained in letter, Hq.,
USSTAF, A.G. 200.6, 3 April 1944, subject, "Awards and Decorations", the
DISTINGUISHED FLYING CROSS is awarded to the folling named Officer, for
extraordinary achievement, as set forth in citation.
*   *   *   *   *   *   *
    RICHARD J. SCHMIDT, O-746432, 1st Lieutenant, 533 Bombardment
Squadron, 381st Bombardment Group (H), Army Air Forces, United States
Army. For extraordinary achievement, while serving as Pilot of a B17
airplane on a number of of bombardment missions over enemy occupied Continental Europe. Displaying great courage and skill, Lieutenant Schmidt
has materially aided in the sucess of each of these missions. His actions
are an inspiring example for his fellow flyers. The courage, coolness and
skill displayed by Lieutenant Schmidt on all these occasions reflect the
highest credit upon himself and the Armed Forces of the United States.
Home address: 6346 S.E.Stephens Street, Portland Oregon.
*   *   *   *   *   *   *
        By command of Lieutenant General DOOLITTLE:

                                        John A. Samford,
                                        Brigadier General, U.S.A.
                                        Chief of Staff

Official:
Edward E. Toro
Colonel, AGD,
Adjutant General

THE STARS AND STRIPES

Daily Newspaper of U.S. Armed Forces · in the European Theater of Operations

Vol. 4 No. 100 · New York, N.Y.—London, England · Monday, Feb. 28, 1944

Week's 8th AF Tonnage Tops 1st Year's

Nazi Fighter Output Is Cut To Ribbons

Down 80 Pct. in One Type, U.S. Spokesman Asserts After Big Friday Raids

Eighth Air Force heavy bombers, joining 15th Air Force bombers from Italy and the RAF in a furious assault on Nazi fighter-plane production, dropped a greater weight of bombs on Germany last week than in the Eighth's entire first year of operations.

The rising tempo of Allied attacks, climaxed by the destruction of 166 enemy aircraft in Friday's U.S. raids on fighter factories at Regensburg, Augsburg and Furth and a ball-bearing plant at Stuttgart, renewed hope that the Luftwaffe might be beaten before invasion.

Even as the conservative British Air Ministry asserted that repeated night and day attacks were wearing down the Nazi fighter strength and there was "everything to suggest that the enemy's air defenses were struggling against odds," an American officer described in British press accounts as a "high spokesman" of the Eighth Air Force was quoted as saying:

"Since Jan. 1, strategic bombing of Germany by British and American forces has reduced the German two-engined fighter production by 80 per cent, single-engine fighter production by 60 per cent, and in addition 25 per cent of bomber production has been destroyed."

Must Keep It Up

Airmen were quick to point out, however, that Germany possessed "extraordinary recuperative powers" and that the optimistic implications of this statement depended to a large extent on the Allied air forces' ability to maintain bombing at the intensity of that last week.

The American spokesman, whose identity was not permitted to be disclosed, said that the Eighth Air Force dropped 7,935 tons of bombs last week, compared with 7,625 tons dropped in its first year of operation.

"We believe we now have fighter production down to the point where the Nazis can't keep up with combat losses," he was quoted as saying. "We can't help but feel that Germany has lost her last hope of maintaining a successful defense."

Besides marking the dispatch of the greatest fighter force ever sent from Britain—bombers and escorting fighters totaled approximately 2,000 aircraft— Friday's raids also marked the deepest U.S. fighter penetration of Germany, 1,100 miles round-trip to Regensburg. Enemy planes destroyed by Eighth Air Force fighters rose beyond 1,000—more than half of them since Jan. 1.

RAF Follows Up Day Blow

Augsburg, one of the U.S. targets in daylight Friday, also was raided twice Friday night by RAF bombers—the second time last week the British Lancasters and Halifaxes had gone out to follow up a day raid.

Photographs made during and after the daylight raids, ETOUSA headquarters said, showed heavy damage to four Messerschmitt single and twin-engine plants at Regensburg, Augsburg and Furth and to the Stuttgart bearings factory. In addition, at least 75 aircraft were damaged on the ground.

At Augsburg, center of Messerschmitt experimental work and main production plant for the Me410, the Nazi fighter-bomber equivalent of the RAF Mosquito, Fortress bombs damaged at least half the important installations, caused a large explosion and smashed up 26 planes on the ground, the Eighth Air Force said.

The RAF, dropping 1,900 tons in two raids two and a half hours apart in a continuation of Augsburg's first major blasting, started fires that raged out of control.

At Stuttgart, photographs revealed that Fortresses caused severe damage to

(Continued on page 2)

Thanks to the airborne radar carried by pathfinder planes, the bombing is completed above the cloud overcast.
(USAAF)

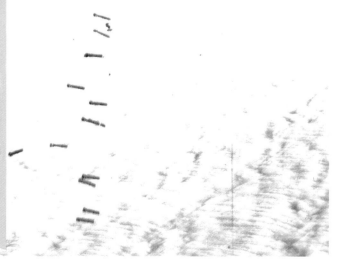

8th AF Tonnage in Week Tops Total in First Year of Bombing

(Continued from page 1)

the Norma ball-bearing works. A large building in the center of the target partially collapsed from high explosive and was set on fire. Several other large buildings were damaged.

Regensburg, home of a large Me109 assembly factory attacked last Aug. 17 by the Eighth Air Force, already was on fire from bombs of the Italian-based 15th Air Force when the Eighth's Fortresses arrived. The plant was heavily hit, every building damaged and a number destroyed by direct hits and fire.

Another formation of Fortresses scored direct hits on at least three and possibly four of the five assembly hangars at nearby Obertraubling, another Me109 assembly plant at Regensburg. Approximately 25 planes were destroyed on an adjoining airfield.

Liberators damaged at least half of the installations at Furth, near Nurnberg, where the target was the Bachmann von

Blumenthal aircraft components plant, believed to be producing for and assembling Me110s and Me410s. High explosive damaged major factory buildings and 24 planes were caught on the ground.

Thirty U.S. bombers were lost in the day's operations. Three fighters failed to return, but 26 enemy interceptors were shot down. The RAF, hammering Augsburg, raiding southwest Germany and the Low Countries with Mosquitoes and carrying out extensive mine-laying, lost 24 aircraft in all operations.

Meanwhile, Marauders of the Ninth Air Force Friday attacked a Luftwaffe base at Venlo, Holland, less than five miles from the German border, and St. Trond airfield in Belgium. At the latter they demolished station headquarters started fires in dispersal areas and scored a direct hit at the intersection of a runway. At Venlo they dropped bombs among aircraft taxi-ing out of dispersal areas to take off and left hangars burning in one corner of the field.

Lt. Schmidt's Missions
21 Feb. - 30 May 1944

Mission 1. Feb 21st, 1944 - Gutersloh, Germany. Duration 7.50 hrs.
Fortresses of the 381st Group flew deep into lower Germany to strike an airfield north of the Ruhr. It was a target of opportunity chosen after primary targets were found hidden under solid cloud cover. Crews reported excellent results. Flak and fighter opposition were both weak.

Mission 2. Feb 25th, 1944 - Augsburg, Germany - 9.45 hrs.
Looming columns of rolling black smoke were visible up to 200 miles from the target today after B-17s penetrated south eastern Germany to strike the Messerschmitt assembly plant at Augsburg. Said lead bombardier 1st Lt. Hendryx: "*Bombing was very good. We knocked out at least three-quarters of the factory. We had a good formation and made an ideal bomb run, laying our bombs in a tight pattern. All we could see was smoke when we turned to head back.*" Two of the group's ship were missing in action.

Mission 3. March 2, 1944 - Frankfurt, Germany - 8.45 hrs.
Industrial installations at Frankfurt were attacked by 35 aircraft of the 381st BG under the command of Major Arthur F. Briggs. The formation found heavy flak in the target area. Enemy fighters were on hand, but their attacks were directed against the formation behind. Bombing was accomplished through 10/10th cloud cover, but an excellent bomb run was made good results likely. One aircraft was lost, Lt. Shultz's is MIA.

Mission 4. March 6, 1944 - Erkner, Germany - 9.00 hrs.
Bombers of the group paid their first visit to Berlin in force, battling their way to the target through hundreds of desperately attacking Nazi fighters. Under the command of Capt. Wood, 30 ships of the 381st BG took part in the operation. Few of the bombardiers had a chance to observe results. Enemy fighters were so thick, that each bombsight man was too busy at his guns to take time to look below. German planes were all of types, many of them firing rockets. Three aircraft of the 381st BG were lost.

Mission 5. March 9, 1944 - Berlin, Germany - 9.45 hrs.
For the second consecutive day, Fortresses heaped devastation upon Berlin with virtually no opposition, dropping tons of explosives through heavy overcast. 29 ships from the group bombed the city under the command of 1st Lt. Sandman, aboard the British-subscribed 'Rotherhithe's Revenge' who reported "*10/10th cloud cover all the way and moderate Flak over Berlin.*" All planes returned safely.

Mission 6. March 16, 1944 - Augsburg, Germany - 9.00 hrs.
Deep attack in Southern Germany, the Fortresses escorted by Allied fighters queued up on industrial targets with virtually no opposition. The Fortress crews saw some German fighters but reported that the Allied escorts kept the Jerries from reaching the bombers, who made the 1,300 mile round trip almost without incident. A fire in the cockpit of a B-17 (serial #42-97454) probably caused by a short circuit caused one of the gunners to bail out over France. The fire under control, Lt. Ducan pulled the bomber back in formation.

Mission 7. March 18, 1944 - Oberpfaffenhafen, Germany - 9.15 hrs.
Vast formations of B-17s penetrated Western Germany almost unopposed today to blast the aircraft factory and adjoining airfield at Oberpfaffenhofen, near Munich. The 381st put up 30 ships into the air to leave their objectives smothered in smoke and flames. In Lt. Schomburg's opinion the mission was highly successful for the 381st. Protected all the way to the target by a 'perfect' fighter escort, the bombers went into their bomb run right on schedule and sent their bombs crashing down on factories, hangars and workshops. All the ships returned safely with no claim or casualty. Flak damage was almost non-existent.

Mission 8. March 20, 1944 - Mannheim, Germany - 9.45 hrs.
Heavy bombers of the 8th AF were over Germany again today, dropping hundreds of tons of high explosives on the southern tip of the Ruhr. Commanded by Major Briggs, 31 aircraft of 381st were airborne. Flak was intense and weather so soupy "*We couldn't see our wingmen.*" Bombing was accomplished through a complete undercast. Results were unobserved. Many of the group's aircraft made the trip home from Germany alone, flying singly in the soup, and never seeing another plane, enemy of friendly. It was a day for the navigators. Most of the pilots flew all the way on

---

533rd Bombardment Squadron (H)
381st Bombardment Group (H)
APO 557

Name Richard J. Schmidt   Rank 1st Lt.   ASN O-746432

Date Asgnd SO/18 Par 2 Hqs AAF Sta 167 21 Jan '44   Combat Hours 305:55

Date	Duty	Target	Time	Pilot	Remarks
Feb 21	CP	Gutersloh, Ger.	7:50	Lt. Townsend	
25	"	Augsburg, Ger.	9:45	" "	
Mar 2	"	Frankfurt, Ger.	8:45	" "	
6	"	Erkner, Ger.	9:00	Lt. Schindler	
9	"	.Berlin, Ger.	9:45	" "	Rec'd Air
16	"	Augsburg, Ger.	9:00	" "	Medal
18	"	Oberpfaffenhafen, Ger.	9:15	" "	
20	"	Mannheim, Ger.	9:45	" "	
22	"	Berlin, Ger.	9:45	" "	
23	"	.Ahlen, Ger.	6:15	" "	Rec'd Oak
24	"	Frankfurt, Ger.	8:15	Lt. McElhare	Leaf Cluster
27	"	St. Jean D' Angley, Fr.	7:45	" "	to AM
28	"	Reims, Fr.	6:30	" "	
29	"	Brunswick, Ger.	8:30	" Townsend	
Apr 18	"	.Berlin, Ger.	9:15	Lt. Townsend	Rec'd 2nd Oak
19	"	Eswege, Ger.	8:00	" "	Leaf Cluster
20	"	Pas De Calais, Fr.	4:50	" "	to AM
25	"	Metz/Frescaty, Fr.	8:15	" "	
26	"	Brunswick, Ger	8:05	" "	
28	"	.Avord, Fr.	7:30	" "	Rec'd 3rd Oak
29	"	Berlin, Ger.	9:35	" "	Leaf Cluster
May 1	"	Troyes, Fr.	6:40	" "	to AM
6	"	Cherbourg, Fr.	6:20	Lt. Eselun	
20	PILOT	Villa Coublay, Fr.	5:50		
22	"	.Kiel, Ger.	7:55		Rec'd the
23	"	Metz/Frescaty, Fr.	8:00		DFC
24	"	Berlin, Ger.	9:30		
25	"	Nancy/Essey, Fr	7:15		
27	"	Ludwigshafen, Ger.	8:15		
30	"	Dessau, Ger.	8:40		Completed Tour

Certified Correct

Karl Franek
Captain, Air Corps,
Operations Officer,

Above.
This document sums up the 30 missions carried out by lieutenant Schmidt between February 21st and May 30, 1944. Schmidt was co-pilot with Lieutenants Townsend, Schindler, Eselun and McElhare, before becoming 1st pilot for his last 7 missions. Medal awards (Air Medal, Oak leaf cluster and DFC) are also mentioned.

Pictured in the cockpit of his B-17, Major George G. Shackley was the 533rd Bomb. Squadron commanding officer.
(USAAF)

This leaflet bearing the number 39 of serial G (Germany) was dropped over Germany during April 1944.

WARNING! FROM PRESIDENT ROOSEVELT TO THE GERMAN PEOPLE

The following declaration was made by president Franklin D. Roosevelt:
"*The United States fights for a world where there is no room for barbarity and violence. They fight for a free world, equal and just. They fight for a world where all men, without distinction or race or religion, may live in peace, honor and dignity. But while we are fighting, Europe and Asia suffer torture and murder. This is the reign of the Nazis and Japanese. Wherever the Nazis or the Japanese rule in terror, they leave to die of hunger and cold, or murder the innocent Polish, Czechs, Norwegians, Dutch, Danish, French, Greeks, Russians and Chinese. The mass-exterminations in Warsaw, Lidice, Kharkow and Nanking are horrible examples of these crimes that are committed everyday and every year, everywhere the Nazis and Japanese have conquered. One of the most terrible crimes in History is the systematic extermination of European Jews. The Nazis began this slaughter before the war; it has only grown bigger in scope since. Hundreds of thousands of Jews, having found refuge in the Balkans and in Hungary to escape the Hitlerian persecutions, are now threatened. This would be a frightful tragedy if these innocent people, who have survived Hitler's rage for ten years, were exterminated on the eve of victory over barbarity. Therefore it is essential to proclaim again our determination: no individual that participates in this crime will remain unpunished. The United States is determined to pursue the guilty ones, and justice will be done. This warning is not only valid for the high officials; it also stands for all executive agents, in Germany and its enslaved satellites, that carry the criminal orders of their superiors. All those that participate in the deportation of Jews, French and Norwegian nationals towards their death in Poland or Germany will be considered as guilty as the executioners, and will not escape their penalty. Hitler commits these crimes against humanity in the name of the German people. I ask all those that live in a country under the German yoke to show the World that they have nothing to do with these insane crimes. I ask you to hide the persecuted victims of Nazi terror, to help them cross the borders and above all to save them from the national-socialist butchers. I demand that you be vigilant and muster the proofs of these crimes, so that these criminals are prosecuted when the day of liberation comes. Thus until Victory the United States will persist to free the victims of Nazi and Japanese brutality. They will employ all the means at hand to locate these victims, without distinction of race or creed. We ask of liberty-loving peoples, in the name of justice and humanity, to unite for this liberation process.*"

The White House, Washington. March 24 1944. Franklin D. Roosevelt, President of the United States of America.

Above.
Inside the nose of a B-17F. Note the ammunition boxes, the pads for the bombardier to lie upon and the chart table on the left. The Norden bombsight is missing from the picture. It was considered as secret weapon and couldn't be photographed.
(USAAF)

Colonel Harry P. Leber, the 381st Bomb. Group CO, pictured in flight gear after a mission.
(USAAF)

instruments and the safe returns were credited largely to the men who handle the maps and compasses.

Mission 9. March 22, 1944 - Berlin, Germany - 9.45 hrs.
B-17s had another crack at Berlin today, dropping hundreds of tons of explosives on the Nazi capital without challenge from a single enemy fighter. The 29 aircraft that made up the 381st formation was under the command of Major Jones, flying aboard 'Georgia Rebel II.' The bombers flew over a 10/10th undercast all the way across Germany. Over Berlin the clouds broke up to some extent, enabling the crews to get a look at their target. In the opinion of the crews it was a "*Perfect mission. Everything went like clockwork*" they said. All ships returned safely.

Mission 10. March 23, 1944 - Ahlen, Germany - 6.15 hrs.
The Luftwaffe made a token appearance today over Germany where hundreds of heavy bombers were again attacking industrial targets. Most of the bomber formations that took part met no enemy fighters throughout the operation. About a dozen Jerries were observed, however, carrying out an attack against a single group of American bombers. The 32 aircraft making up the 381st's contingent were led by Lt-Col. Kunkel, group operations officer. Col. Kunkel said there was a 10/10th overcast over most of Germany, but "*We found a hole in the clouds with a nice big factory sitting under it and we let everything we had go at that.*" The target is believed to have been the factory town of Ahlen, east of Munster. All ships returned, safe and sound.

Mission 11. March 24, 1944 - Frankfurt, Germany - 8.15 hrs.
Weather so thick that it obscured the ground completely and made flying difficult. This failed to prevent American heavies from continuing their attack today, dropping hundreds of tons of explosives on industrial targets in South-east Germany. 23 ships were dispatched by the 381st to take part in the operation. Capt. Douglas L. Winter, who commanded the planes of the group said his formation flew over a solid undercast throughout the mission. A target believed to be Frankfurt was selected for the bombing, but results went unobserved as it was impossible to see below. Three of the 381st aircraft were missing.

Mission 12. March 27, 1944 - Saint-Jean d'Angély, France - 7.45 hrs.
Thirty Fortresses of the 381st BG flew on perfect weather over France to devastate installations of the German-held airfield at Saint-Jean d'Angély, north-west of Cognac. Unhampered by flak or fighters, the bombers were able to carry out precision bombing which reduced the hangars and nearby buildings to fiercely-burning wreckage. All ships returned to base safely.

Mission 13. March 28, 1944 - Reims, France - 6.30 hrs.
Perfect visibility and lack of enemy fighter opposition helped the Fortresses plaster an aircraft factory repair plant on the Reims airfield in France. Under the command of 22-year-old Capt. Franek, 28 aircraft represented the 381st in the operation. Capt Franek said: "*There wasn't a cloud in the sky.*" Several of the ships were damaged by anti aircraft fire, and two crashed in England after their crews bailed out. The lead ship came back with about 50 flak holes.

Mission 14. March 29, 1944 - Brunswick, Germany - 8.30 hrs.
Fortresses of the 381st caught their first glimpse of the Luftwaffe in action in many days when an estimated 150 fighters made a concerted attack on the bomber formation as it swept over Brunswick today. Leader of the 29 ships was the 533rd commander, Major Shackley, aboard a PFF ship, who reported clear weather at his formation's altitude but said bombing results on Brunswick went unobserved because of intervening 8/10th cloud layers below. Attacking enemy fighters were immediately engaged by escorting Allied fighters in violent dogfights after a single pass at the B-17s. Several of the ships returned to base with heavy battle damage.

Mission 15. April 18, 1944 - Berlin, Germany - 9.15 hrs.
Oranienburg, home of the Heinkel plants and only a dozen miles north of Berlin, was the target for Fortresses today and returning crewmen said it was well hit. There were enough American heavies and Allied fighters over Germany to give the men in the B-17s the impression that the attacking force resembled a swarm of locusts over Germany. Capt. Winter commanded the 28 aircraft of the 381st,. The group suffered no fighter attacks and only meager flak.

Mission 16. April 19, 1944 - Eschwege, Germany - 8.00 hrs.
Returning to Germany in great strength, B-17s struck heavily today at the Henschel aircraft works at Eschwege, southeast of Kassel, with good results. Two contingents of 381st bombers took part, comprising 30 aircraft. Colonel Hall who commanded the formation said "*There was a hole in the clouds at Eschwege and we got a good look at the target. We made a 40-second bombing run. The lead bombardier was able to synchronize perfectly and we let our bombs fall in a wide pattern right on the briefed objec-*

Flying headgear as worn on a mission. The officer's service cap has had its stiffening removed as per the current Airforce fashion, it also made it easier to wear the ANB-H1 earphones mounted on the flexible HB-7 headband. The earphones' sonic insulation is ensured by early round-shaped foam rubber earcups. Their rubber material would age quickly and flake off, they were replaced by black hard-rubber oval-shaped components, similar to those fitted on A-11, AN-H-16 and AN-H-15 flying helmets, lined with chamois leather.
The issue AN-6531-1 sunglasses were meant to be used in the plane as well as on the ground. Several sunglasses types were used, either regulation or private purchase.
The pilot also has a T-30 throat mike, and a neck-cloth cut from a parachute shroud. This was typical of crews cruising at high altitudes, because condensation from breathing through the oxygen mask could freeze on the neck area.

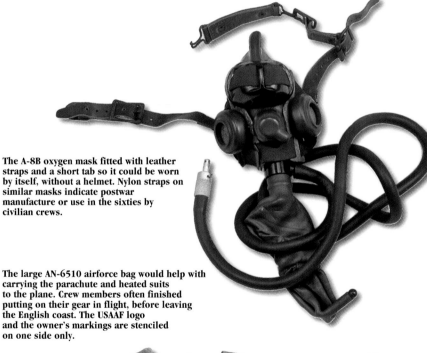

The A-8B oxygen mask fitted with leather straps and a short tab so it could be worn by itself, without a helmet. Nylon straps on similar masks indicate postwar manufacture or use in the sixties by civilian crews.

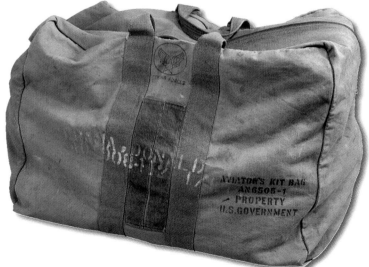

The large AN-6510 airforce bag would help with carrying the parachute and heated suits to the plane. Crew members often finished putting on their gear in flight, before leaving the English coast. The USAAF logo and the owner's markings are stenciled on one side only.

An A-2 flying jacket and close up of its tag under the collar.

TYPE A 2
DRAWING NO. 30-415
A.C. O 42-B7769
PROPERTY
AIR FORCE U.S. ARMY
I SPIEWAK & SONS
NORTH BERGEN, N.J.
38

B-17F pilot, August 1943

August 17, 1943, on Ridgewell airbase, aircrews of the 381st Bomb. Group get ready to board their planes. Target for today is the ball-bearing factory at Schweinfurt in the Munich area. Other units have been assigned the aircraft factories at Regensburg in Southern Germany, near the Alps.

These objectives being out of range on a regular return flight, the planes will fly straight on to North Africa after their bomb run.

This lieutenant has donned an A-4 flying suit with added zippers to close the chest and thigh pockets. In case of an emergency parachute jump, personal items and survival kits would not be lost.

The rough-out leather Pattern 41 flying boots were obtained from the Royal Air Force. These were deemed superior to the AAF A-6 boots. American airmen routinely traded flight gear with their British equivalents.

The A-2 Flying Jacket was worn all through the war, although it had been replaced late in 1943 with cheaper but warmer cotton-shelled jackets such as the B-10, or the B-15 later on.

During high altitude flights, only the pilots and flight engineer would wear the A-2 as their compartment was heated. A pair of A-10 gloves top off our pilot's flying clothing.

A whistle has been hooked to the jacket, a signaling device that would come handy if the plane ditches in water.

The B-3 life vest and the chest parachute AN-6513-1A are essential life saving equipment if the crewman has to bail-out.

If leaving the plane at high altitudes, a small oxygen bottle enables the airman to breathe until he can open his chute. This H-1 bail-out bottle has a constant flow valve, feeding air through a plastic nozzle held between the teeth. The bottle was usually strapped to the thigh as shown, some crewmen would tie it to the chute harness or just slide it inside a boot top.

(Reconstruction, photo Militaria Magazine)

tive." Although the contingent led over the target by Col. Hall met no fighter attacks, an estimated 50 single and twin-engined German fighters made one pass at the group led by 1st Lt. Dorrington.

Mission 17. April 20, 1944 - Pas-de-Calais, France - 4.50 hrs.
A force of 33 B-17s were dispatched by the 381st to attack targets on the French coast. However, bad weather obscured the targets and the formation – confirming the Eighth Air Force policy of discriminate bombing in occupied countries – returned to base without dropping bombs.

Mission 18. April 25, 1944 - Metz/Frescaty, France - 8.15 hrs.
Fortresses again attacked the German-held airfield at Metz (France), 20 miles from the German border, this morning, destroying a number of Nazi planes on the ground as well as hangars and other installations. 28 aircraft of the 381st were dispatched. The crews reported good bombing results.

Mission 19. April 26, 1944 - Brunswick, Germany - 8.05 hrs.
Continuing an unprecedented series of major air attacks against German targets on the continent, fleets of Fortresses blasted Brunswick today, meeting only weak opposition for the enemy. The 381st dispatched 35 aircraft under the group commander, Colonel Leber, who led the combat wing. Bombing was done through 10/10th undercast and results went unobserved. Flak was encountered at the coast going in, at the target and at the coast on coming out. No enemy fighters were seen during the mission.

Mission 20. April 28, 1944 - Avord, France - 7.30 hrs.
Sweeping in over France on the heels of a returning RAF night-bombing force, B-17's smashed the German-held Avord (France) airfield. Led by Major Jones, 28 aircraft of the 381st BG took part in the operation. One brief encounter with the Luftwaffe was reported by returning crew members. They told of a short attack by an estimated 25 to 30 enemy fighters, both FW 190's and ME 109's, a few minutes after turning off the bombing run. Visual bombing was accomplished and the crews were unanimous in their opinion that the results were good. Hangars, barracks and other buildings surrounding the airstrip were hit and set aflame, and bombs left craters across the runways. 533rd bombardier 2nd Lt. Donnatuono, fling in 'Lucky Me,' said: "*We got the first four hangars. I saw the bombs hit them and the hangars simply disappeared. There was a tremendous flash, then all I could see was debris, dust and smoke.*"

Mission 21. April 29, 1944 - Berlin, Germany - 9.35 hrs.
Fortresses were over Berlin again today, dropping their bombs on the German capital through an 8/10th undercast. There were German fighters in the sky, but none of the groups reported great numbers of them. The only concentrated attack was made against a formation of B-24s flying below the Fortress groups. The 381st supplied 27 aircraft that participated in the attack under command of Lieutenant Colonel Kunkel, who was air commander for the combat wing in today's mission. All 381st ships returned safely, although one landed at another base.

Mission 22. May 1, 1944 - Troyes, France - 6.40 hrs.
The important marshalling yards at Troyes, France, southeast of Paris was the target of 381st Fortresses today, and the 24 bombers roared over the French city without challenge from the enemy. Lt. Bowen reported neither flak nor fighters over the target and only moderate flak at the French coast as the bombers were returning home.

Mission 23. May 6, 1944 - Cherbourg, France - 6.20 hrs.
Large number of Fortresses filled the skies over Germany's Channel wall of defence this morning, wading through intense flak to search in vain for rifts in the solid cloud undercast through which they might drop their bombs on German military installations. The 381st operated two separate contingents. An aggregate of 35 B-17s found the entire target area blanketed under clouds. Because of the Eighth Air Force policy of discriminate bombing of occupied areas, all ships but one returned to base still loaded. The exception was 1st Lt. Thompson, who lost an engine to flak aboard 'Century Note' and he salvoed his bombs over the Channel.

Mission 24. May 20, 1944 - Villacoublay, France - 5.50 hrs
Led by the 533rd commander, Lt-Col. Shackley, 13 Fortresses of the 381st swept across France in clear weather today to bomb the German-held airdrome at Villacoublay, south of Paris, with "excellent results." Col. Shackley flying aboard the B-17 'Rotherhithe's Revenge' reported a complete absence of enemy fighters, meager flak at the target and clear visibility all the way. On their way in the crews had a good look at Paris. Visibility was so good at the French capital that crews could make out the Arc de Triomphe as well as the famous Eiffel Tower.

Mission 25. May 22, 1944 - Kiel, Germany - 7.55 hrs.
Flying Fortresses bombed Kiel today without encountering much opposition, when Major Briggs led the 26 ships of the 381st on the mission. He said: "*The weather was pretty good, although there were patchy clouds all the way. We made an excellent bombing run and our stuff fell in a good pattern. The most impressive thing about the mission was the formation. I could see 250 Forts at one time, all in battle array, and it really was an impressive sight.*" The crews said the American fighter escort was "*right on the ball.*" All the ships returned home safely.

Mission 26. May 23, 1944 - Metz/Frescaty, France - 8.00 hrs.
Fortresses were again over France and Southern Germany today, attacking enemy-held transportation and manufacturing centers as part of the pre-inva-

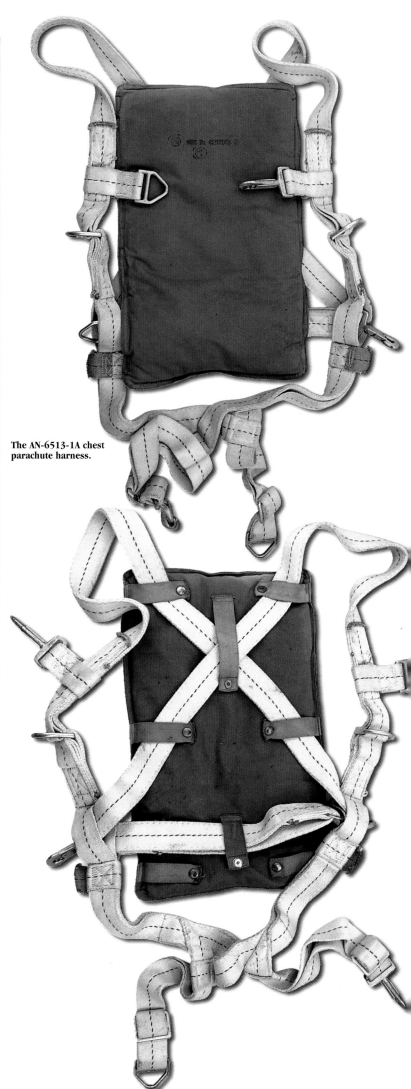

The AN-6513-1A chest parachute harness.

(Continued on page 36)

THE STARS AND STRIPES

Daily Newspaper of U.S. Armed Forces in the European Theater of Operations

Vol. 4 No. 107   New York, N.Y.—London, England   Tuesday, March 7, 1944

Berlin Gets 1st Big Day Bombing

Fierce Battles Rage As Huge U.S. Force Dumps Tons on City

One Fort Division Fights Way In and Out; Other Forts, Libs Meet Few Fighters; Flak Heavy; Weather Better

By Bud Hutton
Stars and Stripes Staff Writer

American heavy bombers attacked Berlin in force yesterday.

With Saturday's attack by a single formation, it was the second U.S. blow in three days on the German capital, and the city's first major daylight assault.

Flanked and covered by relays of Eighth and Ninth Air Force long-range fighters, the Liberators and Fortresses heaped high explosives and incendiaries on their Berlin targets with both visual and "cloud" technique bombing to smash the Nazis' last lingering hopes that any defense could stop the daylight bombers from destroying any objective in the whole Reich.

One division of Fortresses had to slug its way with heavy losses almost every bit of the 600-mile route in to the city, while other divisions reported moderate to almost negligible fighter opposition. Virtually every bomber crew, however, told of intense walls of flak ringing the capital.

There was no official announcement up to last midnight of American losses or claims, but it was expected that the number of bombers reported missing from the day's operations might be among the highest in Eighth Air Force history.

A new record of enemy aircraft destroyed by the escorting fighters also was expected as intelligence officers checked claims and camera gun films.

Mustangs, Thunderbolts and Lightnings, on preliminary reports, probably had outscored the Nazis in the ratio of eight to one and had gone well over the previous single day's score of 61, established on Feb. 22.

While the heavies and their escorts were completing their seventh attack in eight days, a record force of nearly 300 Marauder mediums of the Ninth Air Force carried out heavy attacks on the Nazi airdrome at Beauvais-Tille and military objectives in the Pas de Calais area, all without loss. Sunday night, RAF Mosquitoes had kept the Nazi defenses strained by attacks on western Germany.

With weather conditions obviously much improved over Saturday's when Fortresses dropped the first U.S. bombs on Berlin through almost solid six-mile cloud, Eighth Bomber Command ordered a major, although not record, force to go right back to the same target.

It was scarcely noon when German radio stations began to describe "a gigantic air battle" raging over the Reich from the Zuyder Zee to the capital. Just before 1 PM the sirens began to sound in Berlin.

A few hours later, however, when the blast of bombs and the roar of incendiary-started fires had spread throughout the city, German news agencies put out an official statement admitting damage and casualties from bombs dropped "at random on several residential districts of the town."

Nazi radio stations claimed the Forts and Libs were driven from their targets as they came over the central area of the city, but crews which returned jubilantly to their bases told of pushing home their attacks, in some cases with visual bombing.

Bombardiers picked out individual targets which have survived the 27,000 tons of the RAF's last 15 raids by night and completed their runs while USSTAF fighters held off the Nazi interceptors. Some targets in the capital area were covered, however, and bombardiers used the "through-clouds" technique and could not report results.

Crews from a Fortress group commanded by Col. Edgar M. Wittan, of Newport News, Va., told of "almost endless fights with scores of German planes," and one B17 crew came home to report claims of eight enemy fighters destroyed as an index of the ferocity of the fighting.

The interceptors were hurled at the massed bombers in units of ten and 20, crewmen said, and sometimes "there were

Page One of the March 7, 1944 *Stars and Stripes.* This was the day after the most important aerial battle of all the war, which took place during the first massive daylight raid on Berlin. The 8th AF dispatched around 800 heavy bombers, dropped more than 2.000 tons of bombs and lost 69 bombers and 11 fighters, its heaviest losses of the war. Despite these, the 8th AF was able to return over the city two days later. The Luftwaffe also suffered heavy losses with 67 destroyed fighters, but it never recovered. The Americans' goal had been reached: the capital of the Reich was within their bombing range, the Luftwaffe had been successfully lured into battle and severely battered, many of the downed German pilots were killed.

The article about the March 6th raid relates that three bombers made force landings in Sweden, where their crews were interned (as this country was neutral), bringing the total of American airmen in Sweden to about 130.

Above.
At high altitude, exhausts from plane engines created large contrails which made them easier to spot for German fighters.
(USAAF)

Inset, top.
Map of Berlin and its suburbs. Circled in red, the eastern borough of Erkner was a primary target of the 1st Bomb. Division because of a ball bearings plant. Lieutenant Schindler's plane, with Lt. Schmidt on board, was one of the leading aircraft in the formation.

100 fighters coming at us at once," Lt. Col. Robert M. Tuttle, of Vallejo, Cal., who led one combat wing, said. "We were under attack for five hours, and for two hours the assault was bold and vicious."

Maj. Samuel O. Davis, of Waban, Mass., who led a group in one attack on a Berlin area target, said, "I've never seen such massed air strength as the bombers today. After assembling in line, all you could see was wave after wave of bombers. Wing upon wing swung in a great arc toward the targets in endless procession."

Some groups reported as many as 300 fighters in the air around them at one time, with 30 to 60 fighters in single massed attacks on individual groups.

As the bombers came home and the growing list of losses was classified, it was obvious that once more the Nazis had tried to single out individual formations and concentrate their attacks on them, leaving other units to fly in and out of the Reich almost unmolested.

Bombers from the Fortress group commanded by Col. Kermit D. Stevens, of Portland, Ore., and led yesterday by Maj. Richard H. Cole, of Elizabeth, N.J., reported no more than "25 or 30 enemy aircraft all day," made their bombing runs through ten-tenths cloud and came home without hindrance.

First Mustang pilots back from the attack reported comparatively light opposition over some sections of the city, but the bomber crews' stories of strong resistance.

Meanwhile, Maj. Gen. James Doolittle,

Eighth Bomber chief, sent to Maj. Gen. Lewis H. Brereton, Ninth Air Force leader, congratulations and appreciation for the escort work of the Ninth fighters:

"During the past five days your fighter units have escorted the heavy bombers of this Air Force in a series of penetrations into German territory. These heavy bomber attacks have been increased in effectiveness and our losses greatly reduced by the magnificent support your fighters have rendered. Would you please convey to the pilots and the ground crews of the units concerned my sincere appreciation for the splendid work they have done in our behalf."

Adding his own appreciation to the message, Gen. Brereton sent it on to Ninth Fighter Command groups.

The Berlin assault came after Liberators had pulled Nazi defenses back west with a daylight stab on Sunday to the southwest of France, where they bombed the Luftwaffe base at Cognac, from which many of the long-range anti-convoy raiders take off. Other fields at Bergerac and vicinity also were pounded, while Mustangs, Thunderbolts and Lightnings ran up a 14 to 5 score against German fighters. Thirteen enemy aircraft were shot down by bomber gunners. Four U.S. bombers were lost.

Three U.S. Bombers Down in Sweden

STOCKHOLM, Mar. 6 (AP)—Three American heavy bombers made forced landings at an airport in southern Sweden today and their crews were interned, bringing the total of American airmen in Sweden to about 130.

35

sion blitz. Col. Leber, group commander, was combat wing lead in a pathfinder ship, heading 26 aircraft of the 381st. The formation found an almost complete undercast all the way over France. The primary target was completely covered. Going on to the secondary, the Fortresses found a hole and made a second run over the target to drop their bombs visually. Flak was meager and the formation had no enemy fighter attacks, thus all our ships returned safely.

Mission 27. May 24, 1944 - Berlin, Germany - 9.30 hrs.

The Luftwaffe was up today in attempt to defend Berlin but was unable to stop the large formation of Fortresses from dropping hundreds of tons of bombs on the gutted capital. There was only one brush with the enemy fighters. The commander of the 381st contingent of 39 aircraft said the attack occurred just after the heavy bombers had completed the bombing operation and had turned off the target. *"There were 60 to 70 Jerries"* Col. Fitzgerald said. *"They were coming up from underneath. They climbed out ahead of us then turned back and went for us. They actually came in wing-tip to wing-tip, shooting frantically. They smashed into our high squadron hard. There was only one pass. Our escort was only a few seconds behind them and as soon as our fighters appeared on the scene - that was the end of the fight."* 1st Lt. Clarence Wainwright's plane was shot down. 'Stage Door Canteen,' the B-17 christened a month ago by Mary Churchill, turned in another spectacular performance today, landing back at base with two parachutes acting as brakes. The unusual stopping device was necessary because the big bomber's hydraulic system had been shot out over Berlin, when enemy fighters hit the formation. Loss of the hydraulic system was not the only damage the plane suffered. Five 20-mm shells smashed into the ship, knocking out #3 engine, the radio compass and the oxygen system from the waist to the tail. 1st Lt. Arthur J. Bailey was unable to feather the #3 prop and it windmilled for the rest of the flight, causing 'Canteen' to vibrate wildly. *"We thought even more damage had been done,"* said co-pilot 2nd Lt. John J. Anderson. *"The red stuff from the hydraulic system spurted up into the astrodome, and it looked like blood. We had an idea the boys in the front had been wiped out."* Unable to keep up with the formation, 'Canteen' embarked on the grim task of coming home alone. There were thick clouds and haze all over Germany to make the job of navigation difficult. Once the bomber went off course, passing over Bremen, where *"We got more flak that we saw at the target."* Flak bursts tore about 20 holes in the bomber, but failed to stop it. With 'Stage Door Canteen' hidden from enemy aircraft by the clouds, Lt. Bailey gave the command to lighten the ship, and the crew jettisoned everything moveable except the guns and 50 rounds of ammunition for each fighting position. In the radio room, the waist and tail gunners, their oxygen system cut off, existed precariously by passing round three emergency oxygen bottles. S/Sgt. Charles J. Campbell, Jr., the engineer and top turret gunner, was a busy beaver all the way. The ship had lost all of the gas from the #3 engine, and he was constantly transferring fuel from one tank to another to keep the other three engines turning. Arriving back at home base, Lt. Bailey remembered he had read of another bomber's landing with parachutes for brakes. At his command, Sgt. Alfred Paoli, the tail gunner, pushed a chute out of the tail trap door, while Sgt Coral C. Highsmith performed the same stunt from the waist door. With two chutes floating out behind, the bomber stopped neatly three-quarters of the way down the runway and all the crew climbed out unhurt.

Mission 28. May 25, 1944 - Nancy/Essey, France - 7.15 hrs.

Led by group commander Lt-Col. Harry P. Leber, Jr., the 381st paid another visit to Nancy, France, today. Visibility was good and the Forts made an excellent bombing run. Flak was described as "moderate" and no enemy fighters were seen.

Mission 29. May 27, 1944 - Ludwigshafen, Germany - 8.15 hrs.

Flying Fortresses struck another blow at Ludwigshafen today with both the Luftwaffe and German ground defenses making a desperate effort to stop them. 19 ship of the 381st BG were dispatched but the formation "didn't catch any" of the intense flak barrage over Ludwigshafen and the escorting American fighters kept the Jerries away from making any direct attacks on the group. Dogfights between Allied and German fighters raged all around the formation. However, visibility was good and bombing results were believed to have followed suit.

Mission 30. May 30, 1944 - Dessau, Germany - 8.40 hrs

The large Junkers engine plant at Dessau, southwest of Berlin, took a terrific pounding today from B-17's, which fought their way to the objective through enemy fighter attacks and a skyful of flak. Colonel Gross, combat wing commander, led the 1st Air Division. The fighters, estimated at between 40 and 50, made three head-on passes at the bomber formation. The Jerries were first seen about 40 miles from the target lining up for the attack, their contrails making white patterns high in the sky. They struck just as the Fortresses started on their bombing run, ten Me 109's making the first pass from about 12 o'clock. Two enemy fighters roared through the Fortress pack, when they came so close, Col Gross said, *"it felt like an air bump."* Despite the heavy flak and the harassing fighters, the lead ship made a long, steady bomb run and strike photos show bombs landing right on the aiming point. *"They never tried to fire a gun during the bombing run,"* Col. Gross said, *"In spite of the way the Jerries were swarming all over us. They were there to get bombs on the target and, in spite of Hell, they did."* The fierce enemy fighter attacks exacted their toll, shooting down two ships, Lts. Monahan and Burton's. These two crews were missing in action.

Above.
Inside view of a B-17 fuselage, facing towards the nose, showing the waist gunners' stations and the top part of the ball turret with an oxygen tank.
(USAAF)

Right.
This cartoon by British satirist Giles was pasted in one Lieutenant Schmidt's scrapbooks.

Below.
This May 30, 1944 document (the day of his last mission) rates Lt. Schmidt as "Excellent." He was transferred to a P-38 training unit in the USA. This was his first choice when war had begun.

```
                    Headquarters
            381st Bombardment Group (H) AAF
             Office of the Group Commander
                     APO 557

                                            30 May 1944

201- SCHMIDT, RICHARD J.

SUBJECT: Combat Experience

TO:      Whom it May Concern.

     1.     This is to certify that Richard J. Schmidt, O-746432,
1st Lt. Air Corps arrived in the European Theater of Operations
on 17 December 1943 and has completed his operational tour of
duty as a member of a combat crew on a B-17 aircraft.
     2.     The record of his combat experience is as follows:
            a. Combat Crew Position: Pilot
            b. Number of Operational Missions: Thirty
            c. Date of last mission: 30 May 1944
            d. Number of enemy aircraft destroyed: None
            e. Decorations awarded: Air Medal, three Oak Leaf
               Clusters and Distinguished Flying Cross
            f. Manner of performance of duty: Excellent
     3.     It is recommended that he be transferred to P-38's.


                              _____
                              CONWAY S. HALL,
                              Lt. Colonel. AC
                              Commanding.


201- Schmidt, Richard J.          1st Ind.
HQ, 1st Bombardment Wing (H) APO 557 , 1 June 1944.

To:  Whom it may Concern.
     Approved.


                              _____
                              WILLIAM M. GROSS,
                              Colonel, Air Corps,
                              Commanding.
```

Right.
Lt. Helm's crew was pictured in front of their B-17G back after a mission. Helm is at far right, he and Schmidt were living in the same hut.

Below.
Back in the States, Lt. Schmidt was pictured in the garden of his parents' house in Portland, Oregon.
(RR)

Left.
This telegram was sent by Lt. Schmidt to his parents to inform them that he had safely completed his combat tour.

Below.
1. Hymn and prayer book handed out by the Army, and bearing a 381st BG ink stamp.
2. A-10 flying gloves.
3. 8th Air Force shoulder patch, private purchase in bullion.
4. Chart of Schweinfurt and Munich, published by the British War Office.
5. Pin-up postcard.
6. ID tags.
7. Officer's cap in the '50-mission crush' Airforce style, made by Bancroft. Aviators were partial to its 'Flighter' model, because of its soft construction and fashionable shape.
8. D-3 flight computer.
9. A game set as available at the base PX. The playing cards are still cased and the chess-board could be used to play draughts.
10. AN-6531-1 sunglasses and their case.
11. Pilot wings.
12. Blaisdell crayons for mapping.
13. 'Ruby' brand eraser.

3. 446TH BOMB. GROUP

**705TH BOMB. SQUADRON
1ST LT. ROY H. HOUGHTON
BOMBARDIER
41 MISSIONS - CATERPILLAR CLUB**

The 446th Bomb Group was activated on April 1st 1943 in Arizona and grouped four squadrons (704th, 705th, 706th and 707th BS). The ground echelon embarked on the *Queen Mary* on October 25, 1943 and sailed to England where it arrived on November 2nd. The aircraft left the USA in October, flying the southern Atlantic route from Florida, to Puerto Rico, Brazil, Dakar, and Marrakech (French Morocco) to England, where the group was stationed in Bungay (Station #125), about 90 miles NE of London. Planes of the 446th led the 8th AF on the first heavy bomber mission of D-Day. The 446th operated against strategic objectives on the con-

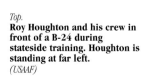

Top.
Roy Houghton and his crew in front of a B-24 during stateside training. Houghton is standing at far left.
(USAAF)

Above.
The 446th Bomb. Group insignia.

Above, right.
Roy Houghton's silver bombardier wings.

Left.
Lieutenant Roy Houghton in England.
(USAAF)

tinent from December 1943 until April 1945. It supported the Normandy landings in June 1944 by attacking strongpoints, bridges, airfields, transportation, and other targets in France. The group also supported ground forces at Caen and Saint-Lô in July by hitting bridges, artillery, and enemy troop concentrations. The group dropped supplies to Allied troops near Nijmegen during the airborne invasion in Holland in mid-September. During the Battle of the Bulge, from December 1944 through January 1945, the 446th struck marshalling yards, bridges and road junctions. It dropped supplies to airborne and ground troops near Wesel during the Allied assault across the Rhine in March 1945. The 446th BG returned to the USA in June/July 1945. The unit was inactivated on August 28, 1945. From December 1943 to April 1945, the 446th BG lost 64 planes during 273 combat missions.

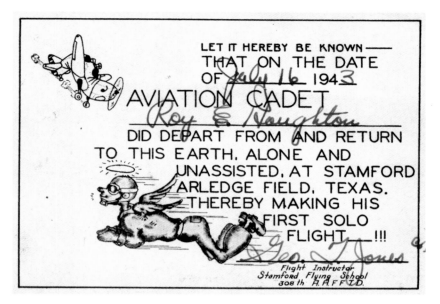

LET IT HEREBY BE KNOWN——
THAT ON THE DATE
OF July 16 1943
AVIATION CADET
Roy E Houghton
DID DEPART FROM AND RETURN
TO THIS EARTH, ALONE AND
UNASSISTED, AT STAMFORD
ARLEDGE FIELD, TEXAS.
THEREBY MAKING HIS
FIRST SOLO
FLIGHT___!!!
Geo. T Jones
Flight Instructor
Stamford Flying School
308th A.A.F.F.T.D.

Above.
Roy Houghton in Aviation Cadet uniform inside a B-24 nose mock-up used for bombsight training. Note the cadet insignia on the lower right sleeve. *(RR)*

Top, left.
Roy Houghton started training as a pilot before being transferred to Bombardier school. He was issued this first solo flight certificate on July 16, 1943. He also drew a pilot log book in which he tallied all his combat missions.

Roy Houghton and family on graduation day. Young ladies are pinning on newly-awarded wings. *(RR)*

Right.
Mug shots from Roy Houghton's escape kit, which would help forging ID papers in occupied Europe.
(USAAF)

Roy Houghton's insignia and awards:
- **British-made Caterpillar Club insignia,**
- **Service ribbons: Air Medal with 5 oak leaf clusters for additional awards, European Theater of - Operations medal with two campaign stars**
- **Dog tag,**
- **Air Medal,**
- **Officer insignia: 1st Lieutenant bars and officer collar badges, all worn in pairs on the service coat.**

Squadron insignia for all four squadrons of the 446th BG. None were authorized by the Army heraldry section.

The 705th Bomb. Squadron insignia.
(USAAF)

The 704th Bomb. Squadron insignia.
(USAAF)

The 707th Bomb. Squadron insignia.
(USAAF)

The 706th Bomb. Squadron insignia.
(USAAF)

Below.
A 706th BS 'box' of Liberators.
(USAAF)

Above.
Roy Houghton's crew at the 446th BG airbase in Bungay (Suffolk). Most of them are wearing the 705th Bomb squadron insignia on their A-2 jackets. Houghton is standing, second from the left.
(USAAF)

Right.
Over the target, B-24s of the 446th BG are dropping their bombs. Smoke plumes are caused by smoke markers planted earlier.
(USAAF)

Above.
**A formation of B-24s
from the 446th BG is flying
over the sea straight
to occupied Europe.**
(USAAF)

Left.
**Armorers are loading a
1000-lb bomb in the
bay of a B-24.**
(USAAF)

Top.
B-24 Liberators of the 446th BG over Tours (France) on June 15, 1944.
(USAAF)

Above, clockwise.
Smoke markers are diving straight to the target: railroad yards and a roundhouse, before bombs hit the bull's eye.
(USAAF)

43

**Maintenance work on a B-24
outer engine.**
(USAAF)

Left.
**A mechanic is checking
the landing gear as
crewmembers are boarding.**
(USAAF)

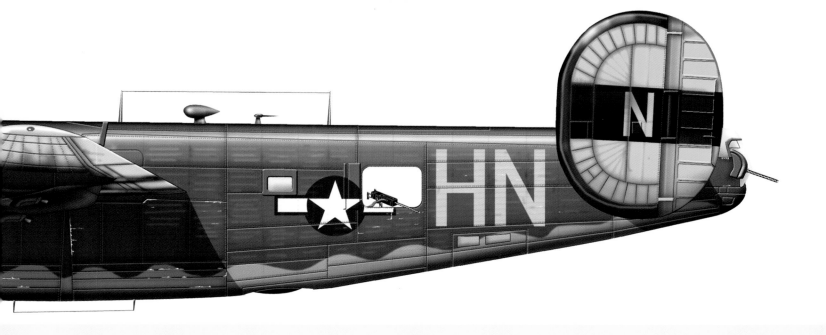

B-24H 'Naughty Nan' (serial# 42-52594) 446th BG/705th BS - September 1944. Lt. Houghton crash-landed on board of this plane on November 12th 1944.
(Computer graphics by Nicolas Gohin)

'Naughty Nan' (serial # 42-52594) from 705th BS was lost after a forced landing on November 12, 1944.
(USAAF)

Right.
B-24s of the 705th Bomb. Squadron flying through a Flak barrage.

Above.
Houghton and his crew are pictured in front of a B-24 named 'Wolf Patrol' on which they flew several missions. Houghton is standing 2nd from left. The plane is aluminum finished in order to save on weight as well as on production time.
(USAAF)

Right.
Another view of 'Wolf Patrol,' taken from Roy Houghton's personal photo album.
(RR)

Left.
**An American Red Cross girl
is serving ice cream to
crewmembers after from
mission.**
(USAAF)

B-24 aerial gunner, March 1944

6 March 1944 on Bungay airfield (Suffolk), 446th BG crews are
boarding their planes.
Target for today is Berlin. The Luftwaffe is expected to put up
quite a show for the occasion and indeed, this raid turned out as a
major battle in the air.

This waist gunner has typical flying gear as worn by 8th AF bomber
crews during the first half of 1944:
– B-6 leather flying helmet with earcups for the R-14 earphones.
While originally fitted with hooks for the A-8B and A-9 oxygen
masks, this particular helmet has received snap fasteners for the
A-10A and A-14 masks
– B-8 goggles with orange-tinted shield
– A-10A oxygen mask with ANB-MC1 microphone
– Rayon neckcloth
– B-4 life vest
– AN-6513-1A chest type parachute and harness, the chest pack is
hand-carried by our man while boarding
– F-2 heated jacket. The cable and jack have been stuck under
a parachute harness strap
– F-2 heated trousers
– F-2 black felt boots
– F-2 heated gloves
– Rayon glove liners.
(Reconstruction, photo by Militaria magazine)

Below.
**Roy Houghton (far left) and other officers of the 446th BG are pictured during
the winter of 1944-45 in England.**
(USAAF)

THE F-2 HEATED SUIT

The F-2 suit remains one of the rarest pieces of USAAF flying gear, even though it was issued in great numbers to bomber crews in the ETO.

The suit was adopted on August 13, 1943, the heat was provided by a 24-volt current; 60.000 sets were delivered.

It superseded the F-1 suit, nicknamed the 'Blue Bunny Suit' (see page 151), on account of its color and because the earlier E-1 12-volt heated suits had been known as 'Bunny suits.'

The new suit featured a sturdier and safer electric resistance that could withstand more than 250.000 flexions without rupturing.

Like most items of Army flying gear, the heated garments bear no manufacturing date on their tags. The only mention is for the year 1938, when the Air Corps first standardized them.

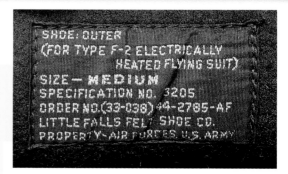

The F-2 outfit is catalogued with regular flying clothing and not with undergarments, like the older suits.

It allows for a greater freedom of movement, which was not the case with previous suits worn under heavy fleece jackets and trousers. The F-2 would protect against the extreme cold encountered at high altitudes, down to minus 90° F.

If the crewman was forced to bail out over enemy territory, the brown serge outer garments could be kept on as warm and inconspicuous clothes.

Like the older heated suits, the F-2 was manufactured by the General Electric Co. and the United Thermo Stable Corp.

The complete F-2 heated outfit is made of six components:
– Heated wool and nylon mix jacket and trouser liners
– Brown serge outer jacket and trousers
– Heated gloves
– Heated felt booties.

The heated liners were buttoned inside the outer garments.

The complete suit proved aleady quite warm before boarding the plane, it was only plugged in at intervals during the flight.

The various heated components are linked together by twin sockets on tabs at the wrist and ankle. The power lead ('pig tail') and plug can be hidden within a small pocket on the jacket's right-hand side.

An additional tab with twin sockets is sewn indide the right hand pocket of the jacket. This was so the E-1 oxygen mask defroster could be plugged in. This appliance also had a socket for the heated shield that could be fitted on the B-8 goggles.

Some F-2 jackets appear to have a lighter-colored imitation fur collar, this would a manufacturer's variation.

F-2 black felt boots were worn over the heated booties. These feature a synthetic rubber sole, and metallic toe box.

The suit was modified in February 1944 as the F2-A, a rheostat was added to its main power cable. The USAAF standardized at the same time the F-3 suit, actually reverting to the previous kind of undergarment that could be worn beneath regular flying clothes.

Above, and above left.
Tags of the F-2 outer jacket and its electrically-heated liner.

The various connecting tabs are visible here, as well as the tab within the chest pocket to plug in the oxygen mask de-icer, and the slit on the side to conceal the main cable and plug. The trouser suspenders are the standard elastic type, also used with the A-8, A-9, A-10 and A-11 flying trousers. Note how the electrical inserts are buttoned in the outer brown serge garments.

The manufacturer's tags for the heated trousers and outer trousers.

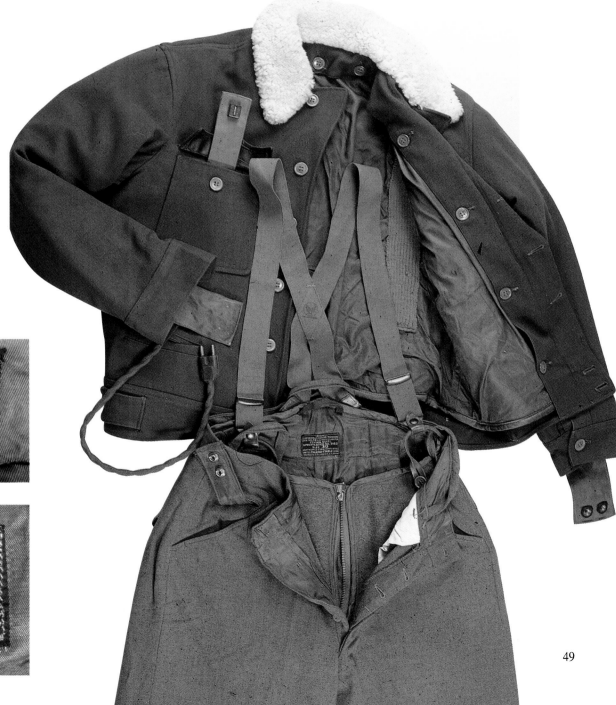

LIEUTENANT HOUGHTON'S LOG BOOK

Houghton, having been commissioned first as a pilot, kept a log book in which he penned all his missions' details.

Mission 1. August 27, 1944 - Oranienburg, Germany - B-24 #184v - duration 5.45 hrs.

The mission was cancelled a hour short of the target, Oranienburg airfield north of Berlin, but crews were credited for a mission.

Mission 2. September 1, 1944 - Beaulieu, France - B-24 #184v - 3 hrs.

This and the subsequent mission to Beaulieu were 'Grocery Runs' during which food and medicine were delivered to liberated France.

Mission 3. September 6, 1944 - Beaulieu, France - Plane not identified - 2.30 hrs.

Same as mission 2.

Below.

Houghton and his crew flew the Northern route to England. They left Topeka, KS on July 10, 1944. Their destination was Grenier Field, NH. From Grenier Field, they flew to Goose Bay, Labrador on the 11th. On the 15th, they flew from Goose Bay to Greenland. On July 21, they flew to Meeks Field, Reykjavik, Iceland. They arrived in Nutts Corner, Ireland on the 22nd. It appears that some time passed between their arrival in the UK and their first operational mission. They were probably waiting to be assigned to their bomb group. There is a blank flight listed by Houghton on 24 August, which was probably their move to the 446th Bomb Group base at Bungay.

Mission 4. September 10, 1944 - Heilbronn, Germany - B-24 'Wolf Patrol' # 42-50882 - 8.45 hrs.

Railyards were attacked with fair results. Lt. Clarence Lloyd's B-24 ('Rough Buddy,' serial #42-95390) was hit by flak and crashed near Strasbourg in France. All crewmen were killed.

Mission 5. September 21, 1944 - Koblenz, Germany - B-24 'Wolf Patrol' - 6 hrs.

Crews were unable to follow the signal given by the PFF plane and missed the target. One plane was hit by Flak (Lt. Goletz) and crash-landed at Bredfield airbase in England, where all the crew was killed. It was their first mission.

Mission 5. September 26, 1944 - Hamm, Germany - B-24 'The Big Drip' #41-29524 - 5.50 hrs.

29 planes of the 446th BG attacked the marshalling yards with fair results. Two planes were lost with their crews:

– 'Temptation' (serial # 42-50477) received multiple flak impacts. Eight parachutes were seen. It was to be this crew's last mission before rotation.

- 'Lil' Max' (serial # 42-100347) was hit by Flak over the target and crashed at Rijswijk in Holland. Pilot and co-pilot were killed (their chutes failed to open), four crewmen were taken prisoner, and five evaded capture.

Mission 7. September 30, 1944 - Hamm, Germany - B-24 # 42-50713 - 6.25 hrs.

26 planes dropped 500 pounders, incendiary bombs and propaganda leaflets, with unobserved results due to cloud cover. Flak at the target was thin and fighter support excellent.

Mission 8. October 2, 1944 - Hamm, Germany - B-24 'The Big Drip' - 6.15 hrs.

The marshalling yards were struck with good results and were seen in flames. Many freight cars were destroyed. Accurate flak damaged to 15 planes out of 38, all returned to base.

Mission 9. October 5, 1944 - Lippstadt, Germany B-24 #42-50713 - 6.45hrs

Several errors caused the 446th BG to miss the target (airfield). One B-24 (Lt. Rust) crash-landed on its return to base.

Mission 10. October 6, 1944 - Hamburg, Germany - B-24 #42-50713 - 6.55 hrs.

The Harburg oil refinery near Hamburg was the target. 31 bombers attacked with poor results. Lt. William Bane (704th BS) was killed by Flak fragments in the abdomen. The co-pilot succeeded in flying the plane back to the base.

Mission 11. October 7, 1944 - Clausthal-Zellerfeld, Germany - B-24 #42-50713 - 7.05 hrs

The target was an explosives factory, which was hit with excellent results.

Mission 12. October 9, 1944 - Koblenz, Germany - B-24 #42-50713 - 7 hrs.

Results of this mission were unobserved. Four German jet fighter contrails were seen, but there was no attack. Fighter cover was very good.

	POINTS OF FLIGHT				AIRCRAFT CLASSIFICATIONS					
					SINGLE ENG. LAND HRS. MIN.		SINGLE ENG. SEA HRS. MIN.		OTHERS SEE TABLE HRS. M	
DATE	FROM	TO	AIRCRAFT MAKE & MODEL	AIRCRAFT REGISTRY						
7-22-44	MEEKS FIELD REYKJAVIK ICELAND	NUTTS CORNER NORTHERN IRELAND	B 24 J						5	1
8-24-44			B-24 H						2	15
8-27-44		ORANIENBURG GERMANY	B 24 J	184V					5	4
9-1-44		BEAULIEU	B 24 H	184V					3	0
9-6-44		BEAULIEU	B 24 J	184V					2	30
9-10-44		HEILBROWN GERMANY	B24J	4250882					8	4
9-21-44		KOLBENZ GERMANY	B 24 H	4250882					6	0
9-26-44		HAMM GERMANY	B 24 H						5	5
					TOTAL		TOTAL		TOTAL	

COPYRIGHTED

	POINTS OF FLIGHT				AIRCRAFT CLASSIFICATIONS					
					SINGLE ENG. LAND HRS. MIN.		SINGLE ENG. SEA HRS. MIN.		OTHERS SEE TABLE HRS. MIN.	
DATE	FROM	TO	AIRCRAFT MAKE & MODEL	AIRCRAFT REGISTRY						
9-30-44		HAMM GERMANY	B 24 J	4250713					6	25
10-2-44		HAMM GERMANY	B 24 H						6	15
10-5-44		LIPPSTADT GERMANY	B 24 H	4250713					6	45
10-6-44		HAMBURG GERMANY	B24H	4250713					6	55
10-7-44		CLAUSTHAL ZELLERFELD GERMANY	B24J	4250713					7	05
10-9-44		KOBLENZ GERMANY	B24H	4250713					7	00
10-10-44			B24J						5	50
10-14-44			B24H						1	30
					TOTAL		TOTAL		TOTAL	

COPYRIGHTED

The 705th Bomb. Squadron insignia.

Below.
Blood chit printed on paper issued to flying personnel involved in 'Frantic' missions during which bombers flew all the way to the Soviet Union after bombing Germany. This document was folded and held in a transparent pocket worn around the neck.

Я американец

" Ya Amerikánets " *(Pronounced as spelt)*

Пожалуйста сообщите сведения обо мне в Американскую Военную Миссию в Москве

Please communicate my particulars to American Military Mission Moscow

Below.
A pathfinder (PFF) ship fitted with a H2-X radar in place of the ball turret is pictured on its way back to England. It is flying on 3 engines, the prop of the far left engine has been feathered. Note the circle marking on the tailfin identifying a PFF ship.
(USAAF)

Above.
Lieutenant Houghton is pictured in England wearing a standard army field jacket with the USAAF patch on the shoulder, and the 705th BS patch on the chest under a leather name tag.
(USAAF)

DATE	POINTS OF FLIGHT FROM	TO	AIRCRAFT MAKE & MODEL	AIRCRAFT REGISTRY	AIRCRAFT CLASSIFICATIONS SINGLE ENG. LAND HRS.	MIN.	SINGLE ENG. SEA HRS.	MIN.	OTHERS SEE TABLE HRS.	MIN.
10-14-44			B 24-J						3	00
10-18-44			B 24J						3	00
10-19-44		MAINZ GERMANY	B 24 J	42 50810					7	00
10-23-44			B 24 H							40
11-5-44		KARLSRUHE GERMANY	B 24 J	4250882					7	35
11-6-44		STERKRADE GERMANY	B24H						2	30
11-9-44		METZ FRANCE	B 24 J	4250888					6	50
11-10-44			B 24 H						2	25
					TOTAL		TOTAL		TOTAL	
				COPYRIGHTED						

Mission 13. October 19, 1944 - Mainz, Germany - B-24 #42-50810 - 7 hrs.

The 446th hit marshalling yards with poor results. Lt. Mullane's 'Slightly Dangerous' was shot down: 3 crewmembers were killed, 7 taken prisoner.

Mission 14. November 5, 1944 - Karlsruhe, Germany - B-24 'Wolf Patrol' #42-50882 - 7.35 hrs

Marshalling yards were the target but because of solid cloud cover results were unobserved. On the way back, Lt. Griffiths landed in France to refuel and reached England at night.

Mission 15. November 6, 1944 - Sterkrade, Germany - plane not identified - 2.30 hrs.

18 planes attacked a synthetic oil plant with unreported results. Flak in the target area was moderate to intense. Two planes received minor battle damage.

Mission 16. November 9, 1944 - Metz, France - B-24 'Wolf Patrol' - 6.50 hrs.

General Patton's ground forces in the Metz area were able to advance after the 446th bombed the German fortresses, with excellent results.

Mission 17. November 11, 1944 - Bottrop, Germany - B-24 #42-50713 - 6.13 hrs.

Target for the day was a synthetic oil plant. The B-24s were faced with intense flak and overall cloud cover.

November 12, 1944 - Non-Bombing Flight - B-24 'Naughty Nan' #42-52594 - 1.10 hr.

Mission was aborted. Houghton recorded in his log book that he "Cracked up Naughty Nan," probably due to an engine failure. The 446th BG went on a 9 day stand-down for airfield repairs.

Mission 18. November 21, 1944 - Hamburg, Germany - B-24 #42-50810 - 7.15 hrs.

A synthetic oil refinery was the target. The crews met with intense flak. 'Satan's Little Sister' (serial # 42-95180 - Lt. Quinn) was hit. The crew tried to bail out over Holland, there were only two survivors.

Mission 19. November 25, 1944 - Bingen, Germany - B-24 #42-50713 - 7.30 hrs

Marshalling yards were attacked by 38 planes of the group. Observed results were good.

Mission 20. November 29, 1944 - Bielefeld, Germany - B-24 #42-50713 - 6.40 hrs.

The B-24s returned over a railway viaduct that had been struck with poor results, most of the bombs falling short. There were hits in the target area, although many of the bombs fell to the left.

Mission 21. December 2, 1944 - Bingen, Germany - B-24 #42-50713 - 6.30 hrs.

33 planes attacked the marshalling yards through clouds with unobserved results. Two planes were lost for unknown reasons, the heavy clouds masking their fate from other crews: 'She's Mine' (# 42-95105) and 'Tiger' (# 42-51100). All 21 men died.

There was no Flak, fighter support was excellent and no enemy fighters were seen. Houghton records: *"Stalled out on bomb run. Returned alone."*

Mission 22. December 6, 1944- Minden, Germany - B-24 #42-50713 - 6.45 hrs.

Twenty-eight 446th BG planes targeted a viaduct. Nine others attacked a rail junction as a secondary target when they could not form up with the main group. Some crews reported hits in open fields between the viaduct and the town.

Mission 23. December 12, 1944 - Hanau, Germany - Plane not identified - 4.40 hrs.

Marshalling yards were attacked with good results. The crew of Lt. Christensen flying 'Wedding Belle' (serial # 42-95178) was lost on the mission after ditching in the sea.

Above.
The two flights on October 14th and 18th, of same duration, were apparently training flights.

DATE	POINTS OF FLIGHT FROM	TO	AIRCRAFT MAKE & MODEL	AIRCRAFT REGISTRY	AIRCRAFT CLASSIFICATIONS SINGLE ENG. LAND HRS.	MIN.	SINGLE ENG. SEA HRS.	MIN.	OTHERS SEE TABLE HRS.	MIN.
11-11-44		BOLTROP WELLEIM GERMANY	B 24J	4250713					6	15
11-12-44			B 24J	427594					1	10
11-21-44		HAMBURG GERMANY	B 24J	4250810					7	15
11-25-44		BINGEN GERMANY	B 24J	4250713					7	30
11-29-44		BEILEFELD GERMANY	B 24J	4250713					6	40
12-2-44		BINGEN GERMANY	B 24J	4250713					6	30
12-6-44		MINDEN GERMANY	B 24J	4250713					6	45
12-18-44		HADRU	B 24H						4	40
					TOTAL		TOTAL		TOTAL	
				COPYRIGHTED						

Above.
This photo was taken on September 30, 1944 during a raid over Hamm in Germany, 26 planes of the 446th BG were committed. White plumes have been caused by the condensation from an earlier 'box' and smoke markers.
(USAAF)

Below.
At the beginning of September 1944, tons of food and medicine were ferried to the recently liberated French people. Empty bombers of the 446th BG left Bungay to get loaded at another base in England. They were then flown to airfields in France such as Orléans-Bricy or Beaulieu. The runways were in such bad shape that engineers had to rebuild them first. The crews were met with open arms by the French, who helped unload the planes. Here, ships of the 446th BG are loaded with flour bags by RAF personnel somewhere in Southern England.
(USAAF)

POINTS OF FLIGHT					AIRCRAFT CLASSIFICATIONS					
					SINGLE ENG. LAND		SINGLE ENG. SEA		OTHERS SEE TABLE	
DATE	FROM	TO	AIRCRAFT MAKE & MODEL	AIRCRAFT REGISTRY	HRS.	MIN.	HRS.	MIN.	HRS.	MIN.
12-22-44			B24H						5	30
12-25-44		MÜRLENBACH GERMANY	B24J	427576					4	30
12-27-44		KAIZERLAUTERN GERMANY	B24J	4250713					6	00
12-30-44		MECHERNICH GERMANY	B24J	4250713					6	40
12-31-44			B24J						1	40
1-7-45			B24J						4	00
1-8-45		CLERF LUXEMBURG	B24J	4250713					5	15
1-15-45		REUTLINGEN GERMANY	B24J	4250713					8	35
				450.		TOTAL		TOTAL		TOTAL

COPYRIGHTED

December 22, 1944 - No Target listed - 5.30 hrs.
No combat mission for the 446th BG on the date, this was probably a training flight.

Mission 24. December 25, 1944 - Murlenbach, Germany - B-24 #42-7576 - 4.30 hrs.
Rail yards were attacked by 30 planes with good results. It was a visual aiming mission.

Mission 25. December 27, 1944 - Kaiserslautern, Germany - B-24 #42-50713 - 6 hrs.
18 planes hit a rail bridge with fair results and 7 more hit Enkenbach as target of opportunity. The plane piloted by Lt. Andrews (serial # 42-50330) crashed on takeoff, killing him. Another one (serial # 42-50491) piloted by Lt. Malone was forced to ditch into the Channel. Seven crewmen were killed, the three other were rescued. A third plane (serial # 42-51312 - Lt. Whaley) was hit by Flak while in the target area. The crew was forced to bail out, 6 were taken prisoner, 4 escaped. A fourth crew was also forced to bail out ('Shoo Shoo Baby' serial # 42-52747, Lt. Woodburn) near Brussels in Belgium, due to engine problems. All landed safely, several with a broken leg.

Mission 26. December 30, 1944 - Mechernich, Germany - B-24 #42-50713 - 6.40 hrs.
Six planes attacked a rail yards with unobserved results. Houghton notes: " *Lost prop on #1 engine. Salvoed bombs - on landing slid 90 degrees for 150 feet.*"

December 31, 1944 - No target listed - 1.40 hrs.
No target listed. Mission probably aborted.

January 7, 1945 - No target listed - 4 hrs
No target listed. Mission probably aborted.

Mission 27. January 8, 1945 - Clervaux, Luxembourg - B-24 #42-50713 - 5.15 hrs
A road junction was bombed by 16 planes with unobserved results. Houghton and crew must have experienced trouble as they landed at Lille, France.

Mission 28. January 15, 1945 - Reutlingen, Germany - B-24 #42-50713 - 8.35 hrs.
Marshalling yards were hit by 34 planes with good results. One plane landed on the Continent low on gasoline.

Mission 29. January 16, 1945 - Ruhland, Germany - B-24 #42-50713 - 9.15 hrs
The Lauta aluminum plant was bombed with satisfactory results. Lt. Griffith's plane was hit by flak, the port side fuel tank and hydraulic system were shot, gasoline was streaming back so fast through the bomb bay that smoke appeared. The B-24 landed on the Continent. Most of the planes landed in Yorkshire because they were low on gas. This mission took over nine hours, the second longest mission Houghton flew.

January 21, 1945 - Ruhland - B-24 #42-50713 - 4 hrs.
Target was Heilbronn. However, high clouds made it impossible to form and the flight was recalled. Two planes (Lts. Kerns and Roberts) tagged along with 491st BG planes into Heilbronn. Results there went unobserved.

Mission 30. January 29, 1945 - Munster, Germany - B-24 #42-50713 - 5.40 hrs
Thirty eight planes attacked the marshalling yards through 10/10 cloud cover.

Mission 31. January 31, 1945 - Brunswick, Germany - B-24 #42-50713 - 8.15 hrs.

This mission was cancelled shortly before the target run but under the new Division rules, the Group received credit. Houghton records that his plane lost No 2 engine over Dummer Lake. Located just west of Hannover, the lake was a navigational landmark for the 8th AF. But the Germans soon realized this and covered the area with flak batteries. On the return leg of the mission, it must have become apparent that the B-24 would not make it back to base. The entire crew bailed out over Cambridge. Houghton thus became a member of the 'Caterpillar Club' (its badge is shown on page 38) as a result of his chute saving his life.

Mission 32. February 9, 1945 - Magdeburg, Germany - Plane not identified - 7.30 hrs.
Marshalling yards were the target. Unobserved results. Houghton recorded this mission as Brunswick but the 446th BG history indicates Magdeburg.

February 10, 1945 - Magdeburg - No plane identified - 0.30 hr.
Due to the expected flight duration, Houghton's crew turned back to England for unknown reasons.

Mission 33. February 14, 1945 - Magdeburg, Germany - B-24 #42-50356 - 7.30 hrs.
Thirty-one planes hit the marshalling yards with unobserved results. Houghton reports that their B-24 lost No 3 engine over the Initial Point at Kassel.

Mission 34. February 17, 1945 - Gera, Germany - B-24 #751 - 4.30 hrs.
The 446th BG history shows no mission flown on this date. Houghton probably made an error filling his log book.

POINTS OF FLIGHT					AIRCRAFT CLASSIFICATIONS					
					SINGLE ENG. LAND		SINGLE ENG. SEA		OTHERS SEE TABLE	
DATE	FROM	TO	AIRCRAFT MAKE & MODEL	AIRCRAFT REGISTRY	HRS.	MIN.	HRS.	MIN.	HRS.	MIN.
1-16-45		RUHLAND GERMANY	B24J	4250713					9	15
1-21-45		RUHLAND	B24J	4250713					4	00
1-29-45		MUNSTER GERMANY	B24J	4250713					5	40
1-31-45		BRUNSWICK GERMANY	B24J	4250713					8	15
2-9-45			B24J						7	30
2-10-45			B24H							30
2-14-45		MAGDEBURG GERMANY	B24H	4250356					7	30
2-17-45		GERA GERMANY	B24H	751					4	30
						TOTAL		TOTAL		TOTAL

COPYRIGHTED

On these two photos, ships of the 446th BG are loaded with flour bags by RAF personnel somewhere in Southern England. These were part of shipments for the French population.

Mission 35.
February 22, 1945 - Northeim, Germany - B-24 #42-50365 - 5.10 hrs.

The roundhouse was completely destroyed. The marshalling yard and tracks were also targeted with excellent results. The 446th planes flew as part of a massive force, bombing from exactly 8.000 feet. On the way back, they encoutered RAF bombers going in. Visibility was perfect.

Mission 36.
February 23, 1945 - Osnabruck, Germany - B-24 #42-50751 - 9.30 hrs.

The city of Osnabruck was raided after the primary target, the Gera marshalling yards, was bypassed due to adverse weather conditions.

Mission 37. February 24, 1945 - Misburg, Germany - B-24 #42-50629 - 6 hrs.

Unobserved results for this mission, later reports however mentioned that the oil refinery had been hit.

Mission 38. March 8, 1945 - Betzdorf, Germany - B-24 #42-500751 - 6.35 hrs.

Eighteen planes attacked the marshalling yards with unobserved results.

Mission 39. March 10, 1945 - Paderborn, Germany - B-24 #42-50059 - 7.50 hrs.

DATE	FROM	TO	AIRCRAFT MAKE & MODEL	AIRCRAFT REGISTRY	SINGLE ENG. LAND HRS.	MIN.	SINGLE ENG. SEA HRS.	MIN.	OTHERS SEE TABLE HRS.	MIN.
2-22-45		NORTHIEM GERMANY	B24H	4250365					5	10
2-23-45		GERA GERMANY	B24J	4250751					9	30
2-24-45		MISBURG GERMANY	B24J	4250629					6	00
3-8-45		BETZDORF GERMANY	B24J	4250751					6	35
3-10-45		PADERBORN GERMANY	B24H	4250059					7	50
3-11-45		KIEL GERMANY	B24J	4250365					7	35
3-12-45		SWINEMUNDE GERMANY	B24J	4250810					8	25
5-29-45	HOMESTEAD FLORIDA	LOCAL	C54A						4	05
					TOTAL		TOTAL		TOTAL	

COPYRIGHTED

During the winter of 1944, Roy Houghton is in full flight gear in front of his ship. He has donned an A-2 jacket over a AN-6550 flying suit and probably an F-3 heated outfit. His gloves are the RAF pattern 41, the rest of his gear are: an A-11 leather flying helmet with AN -6530 goggles, an A-14 an oxygen mask and the A-3 parachute.
(RR)

Thirty three B-24s bombed the marshalling yards.

Results were unobserved over a solid undercast.

Mission 40. March 11, 1945 - Kiel, Germany - B-24 #42-50365 - 7.35 hrs.

The submarine yards were hit thanks to H2X radar aiming, with unobserved results

Mission 41. March 12, 1945 - Swinemunde, Germany - B-24 # 42-50810 - 8.25 hrs.

The 446th BG led a 675-plane formation on the Baltic port city of Swinemunde to support Soviet ground troops. Harbor installations were hit with excellent results.

This was Houghton's final combat mission.

Taken from the tail turret of a B-24, this photo shows planes of the 446th BG flying through a Flak barrage near the target, as white trails left by smoke markers can be observed.
(USAAF)

Above.
446th BG crews are waiting for instructions before boarding their planes.
(USAAF)

Right.
Roy Houghton posing in front of 'Wolf Patrol,' on which he flew four missions.
(RR)

457th Bomb Group

4. 457TH BOMB. GROUP

749TH BOMB. SQUADRON
STAFF SGT. THOMAS D. DALRYMPLE
GUNNER
INTERNEE IN SWITZERLAND

The 457th Bomb. Group Insignia.

The 457th Bombardment Group, consisting of the 748th, 749th, 750th and 751st Bombardment Squadrons, was activated on July 1, 1943. On January 4, 1944, Col. James R. Luper took over as Commanding Officer from Lt.-Col. Hugh O. Wallace who had led the Group during the training phase. The 457th BG ships left the USA on January 17, 1944, flying individually to England.

The new 457th BG airfield (Station 130) was located near Glatton, a small village not far away from Polebrook (351st BG) and Deenethorpe (401st BG). February 1944 was spent training while Colonel Luper and several other officers flew on combat missions with other groups. Finally, the Group was deemed ready and alerted for their first mission on February 14th 1944. The mission, however, was scrubbed before takeoff. The 457th Bomb Group entered combat just in time for the 'Big Week.'

On February 21st 1944, the 457th dispatched 36 aircraft to attack Gutersloh and Lippstadt. The bombing results were poor, and the Group sustained its first aircraft/crew loss. During the week, three aircraft were lost to the enemy, another was lost on landing and three more aircraft made it

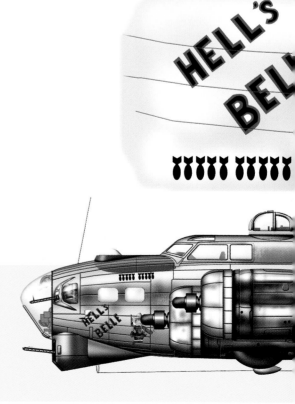

back to England badly damaged. Following the Big Week, the March 6, 1944 mission to Berlin saw the 8th Air Force's largest effort yet against the enemy capital. Preparations for the invasion began in April 1944, many missions were flown against French targets, notably airfields. On April 9th, the FW-190 fighter assembly complex in Gdansk, Poland was attacked with heavy losses for the 457th, however with excellent results. The 457th lost four aircraft and eleven crew members were killed. As D-Day neared, more and more missions on tactical targets in France and Belgium were flown, along with missions to Germany: over Berlin (5 times in May), Lutzkendorf, Ludwigshafen, Dessau and Oscherleben. Targets in France, mostly airfields and railways, were hit early in June, on D-Day, and all through June. On June 14th, the 457th attacked Melun airfield near Paris with poor bombing results and lost five aircraft and 43 crew members (KIA/MIA).

Between June and December 1944, the 457th flew many missions against opposition ranging from nil to terrifying. Some notably rugged missions were:

– Magdeburg on September 28th 1944, 7 aircraft were lost, 15 damaged, 63 crew members were listed as KIA/MIA

– Merseberg on November 2nd 1944, 9 aircraft were lost, 9 damaged, 82 crew members KIA/MIA.

Of the personnel listed as KIA/MIA, few were actually killed or missing, most survived as POWs. On October 8, 1944, Colonel Harris E. Rogner replaced Col. Luper (who had been captured) as Group Commanding Officer. Throughout the fall of 1944 German fighters remained active, but the 457th did not suffer more devastating losses. Weather at the turn of the year was abysmal, but with improved radar bombing, the 8th Air Force stepped up its missions against oil, transport and industrial targets. On March 18th, the 457th was attacked by Me-262 jet fighters over Berlin. In March 1945, the 8th Air Force dropped a greater tonnage of bombs on Germany than it had the previous months combined.

The 457th BG flew its last mission on April 20th 1945. On June 4, 1945, aircraft of the 457th began flying back to the United States. Ground personnel boarded the *Queen Elizabeth* in Glasgow, bound for New York City. The 457th BG was disbanded on August 18th 1945, as many other heavy bomb groups of the 8th AF. Colonel Luper survived POW camp, and returned home. From February 1944 to May 1945, the unit lost 83 planes, for a total of 236 missions.

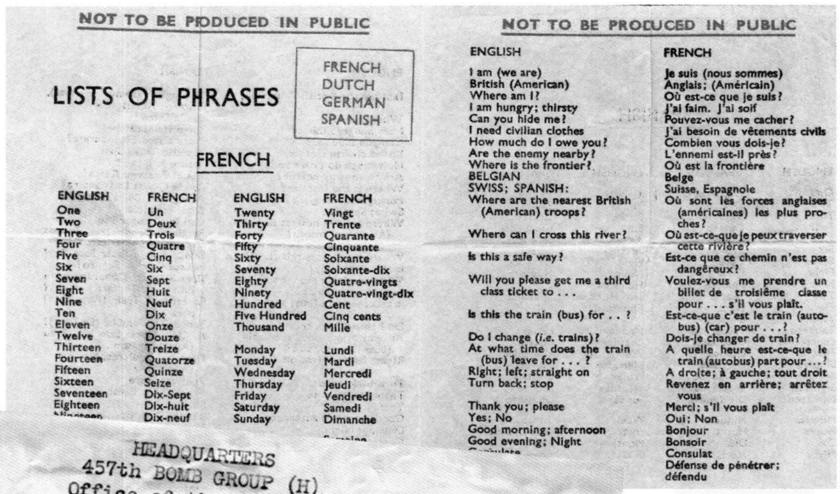

NOT TO BE PRODUCED IN PUBLIC

LISTS OF PHRASES

FRENCH
DUTCH
GERMAN
SPANISH

FRENCH

ENGLISH	FRENCH	ENGLISH	FRENCH
One	Un	Twenty	Vingt
Two	Deux	Thirty	Trente
Three	Trois	Forty	Quarante
Four	Quatre	Fifty	Cinquante
Five	Cinq	Sixty	Soixante
Six	Six	Seventy	Soixante-dix
Seven	Sept	Eighty	Quatre-vingts
Eight	Huit	Ninety	Quatre-vingt-dix
Nine	Neuf	Hundred	Cent
Ten	Dix	Five Hundred	Cinq cents
Eleven	Onze	Thousand	Mille
Twelve	Douze		
Thirteen	Treize	Monday	Lundi
Fourteen	Quatorze	Tuesday	Mardi
Fifteen	Quinze	Wednesday	Mercredi
Sixteen	Seize	Thursday	Jeudi
Seventeen	Dix-Sept	Friday	Vendredi
Eighteen	Dix-huit	Saturday	Samedi
Nineteen	Dix-neuf	Sunday	Dimanche

NOT TO BE PRODUCED IN PUBLIC

ENGLISH	FRENCH
I am (we are)	Je suis (nous sommes)
British (American)	Anglais; (Américain)
Where am I?	Où est-ce que je suis?
I am hungry; thirsty	J'ai faim. J'ai soif
Can you hide me?	Pouvez-vous me cacher?
I need civilian clothes	J'ai besoin de vêtements civils
How much do I owe you?	Combien vous dois-je?
Are the enemy nearby?	L'ennemi est-il près?
Where is the frontier?	Où est la frontière?
BELGIAN:	Belge
SWISS; SPANISH:	Suisse, Espagnole
Where are the nearest British (American) troops?	Où sont les forces anglaises (américaines) les plus proches?
Where can I cross this river?	Où est-ce-que je peux traverser cette rivière?
Is this a safe way?	Est-ce que ce chemin n'est pas dangereux?
Will you please get me a third class ticket to . . .	Voulez-vous me prendre un billet de troisième classe pour . . . s'il vous plaît.
Is this the train (bus) for . . ?	Est-ce-que c'est le train (autobus) (car) pour . . .?
Do I change (i.e. trains)?	Dois-je changer de train?
At what time does the train (bus) leave for . . . ?	A quelle heure est-ce-que le train (autobus) part pour . . .?
Right; left; straight on	A droite; à gauche; tout droit
Turn back; stop	Revenez en arrière; arrêtez vous
Thank you; please	Merci; s'il vous plaît
Yes; No	Oui; Non
Good morning; afternoon	Bonjour
Good evening; Night	Bonsoir
	Consulat
	Défense de pénétrer; défendu

Above and bottom, left.
This language flash card, printed on very thin blue paper, was handed out together with WD pamphlet No 21-7 *"If you should be captured"* to all aircrew members shortly before D-Day.

Bottom left.
2nd part of the card, relating to Dutch conversation. Other side of document is printed with German and Spanish phrases.

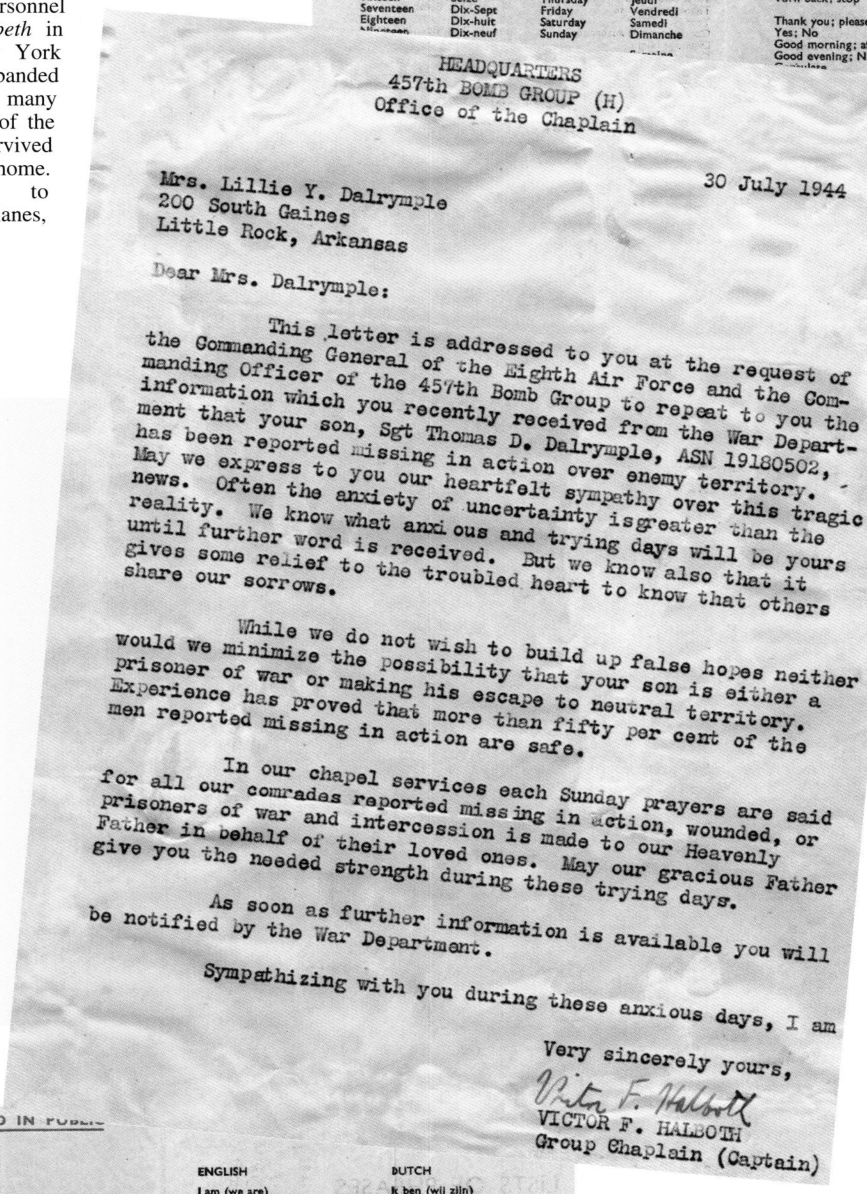

HEADQUARTERS
457th BOMB GROUP (H)
Office of the Chaplain

30 July 1944

Mrs. Lillie Y. Dalrymple
200 South Gaines
Little Rock, Arkansas

Dear Mrs. Dalrymple:

This letter is addressed to you at the request of the Commanding General of the Eighth Air Force and the Commanding Officer of the 457th Bomb Group to repeat to you the information which you recently received from the War Department that your son, Sgt Thomas D. Dalrymple, ASN 19180502, has been reported missing in action over enemy territory. May we express to you our heartfelt sympathy over this tragic news. Often the anxiety of uncertainty is greater than the reality. We know what anxious and trying days will be yours until further word is received. But we know also that it gives some relief to the troubled heart to know that others share our sorrows.

While we do not wish to build up false hopes neither would we minimize the possibility that your son is either a prisoner of war or making his escape to neutral territory. Experience has proved that more than fifty per cent of the men reported missing in action are safe.

In our chapel services each Sunday prayers are said for all our comrades reported missing in action, wounded, or prisoners of war and intercession is made to our Heavenly Father in behalf of their loved ones. May our gracious Father give you the needed strength during these trying days.

As soon as further information is available you will be notified by the War Department.

Sympathizing with you during these anxious days, I am

Very sincerely yours,

VICTOR F. HALBOTH
Group Chaplain (Captain)

Right.
Dated 30 July 1944, this tragic letter was sent by the 457th BG chaplain to Mrs. Dalrymple (S/Sgt Dalrymple's mother) to inform her that her son had been reported MIA.

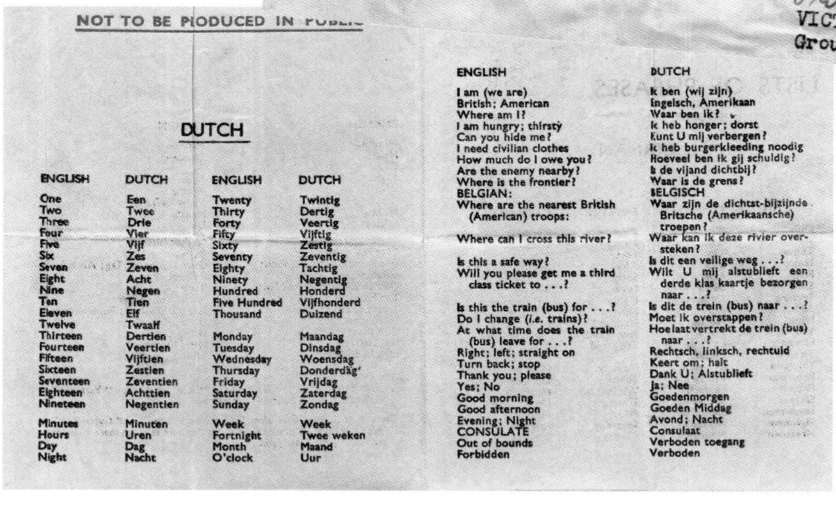

NOT TO BE PRODUCED IN PUBLIC

DUTCH

ENGLISH	DUTCH	ENGLISH	DUTCH
One	Een	Twenty	Twintig
Two	Twee	Thirty	Dertig
Three	Drie	Forty	Veertig
Four	Vier	Fifty	Vijftig
Five	Vijf	Sixty	Zestig
Six	Zes	Seventy	Zeventig
Seven	Zeven	Eighty	Tachtig
Eight	Acht	Ninety	Negentig
Nine	Negen	Hundred	Honderd
Ten	Tien	Five Hundred	Vijfhonderd
Eleven	Elf	Thousand	Duizend
Twelve	Twaalf		
Thirteen	Dertien	Monday	Maandag
Fourteen	Veertien	Tuesday	Dinsdag
Fifteen	Vijftien	Wednesday	Woensdag
Sixteen	Zestien	Thursday	Donderdag
Seventeen	Zeventien	Friday	Vrijdag
Eighteen	Achttien	Saturday	Zaterdag
Nineteen	Negentien	Sunday	Zondag
Minutes	Minuten	Week	Week
Hours	Uren	Fortnight	Twee weken
Day	Dag	Month	Maand
Night	Nacht	O'clock	Uur

ENGLISH	DUTCH
I am (we are)	Ik ben (wij zijn)
British; American	Ingelsch, Amerikaan
Where am I?	Waar ben ik?
I am hungry; thirsty	Ik heb honger; dorst
Can you hide me?	Kunt U mij verbergen?
I need civilian clothes	Ik heb burgerkleeding noodig
How much do I owe you?	Hoeveel ben ik gij schuldig?
Are the enemy nearby?	Is de vijand dichtbij?
Where is the frontier?	Waar is de grens?
BELGIAN:	BELGISCH
Where are the nearest British (American) troops?	Waar zijn de dichtst-bijzijnde Britsche (Amerikaansche) troepen?
Where can I cross this river?	Waar kan ik deze rivier oversteken?
Is this a safe way?	Is dit een veilige weg . . .?
Will you please get me a third class ticket to . . .?	Wilt U mij alstublieft een derde klas kaartje bezorgen naar . . .?
Is this the train (bus) for . . .?	Is dit de trein (bus) naar . . .?
Do I change (i.e. trains)?	Moet ik overstappen?
At what time does the train (bus) leave for . . .?	Hoe laat vertrekt de trein (bus) naar . . .?
Right; left; straight on	Rechtsch, linksch, rechtuid
Turn back; stop	Keert om; halt
Thank you; please	Dank U; Alstublieft
Yes; No	Ja; Nee
Good morning	Goedenmorgen
Good afternoon	Goeden Middag
Evening; Night	Avond; Nacht
CONSULATE	Consulaat
Out of bounds	Verboden toegang
Forbidden	Verboden

Interned in Switzerland

Switzerland, as a neutral country, did not suffer unduly during World War II, but came to be reluctantly involved. The Swiss Flugwaffe and Anti-Aircraft Artillery had to protect its airspace from intruders and so they did.

The first were 'stray' Luftwaffe aircraft who attempted to provoke the Swiss and on several occasions, Swiss Me-109 shot down their German stable-mates!

In 1942 began the strategic bombardment campaign against the Ruhr valley, and Allied planes started to crash or land in Switzerland. The first were RAF aircraft (12 in all) but by the beginning of 1943, daylight missions of the USAAF against Germany started, and 160 US planes would crash or land in Switzerland.

(Continued on page 62)

Right.
The Regina hotel in Wengen, where S/Sgt. Dalrymple and his crewmates were detained. The living conditions for American internees in Switzerland were indeed uncommon… (back of this postcard however, Dalrymple scribbled *"Nice Place but No Food."*). *(RR)*

When you are questioned, by no matter what enemy authority, you must give only your name, rank, and serial number. Beyond that, there is no information which the enemy can legally force from you.

Do not discuss military matters of any sort with anyone.

An "Allied" soldier may be an enemy intelligence agent.

Forget all you ever knew about your own Army. If anyone wants to discuss it with you, even its insignificant details, say nothing.

7

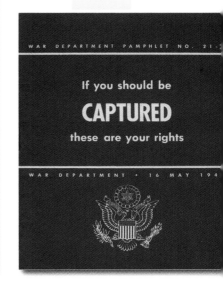

WAR DEPARTMENT PAMPHLET NO. 21-

If you should be

CAPTURED

these are your rights

WAR DEPARTMENT • 16 MAY 194

From the moment you are captured you have certain rights. Even before you are taken to a prisoner-of-war camp, these rights are in effect.

Stand up for your rights, but do it with military courtesy and firmness at all times. The enemy will respect you for it.

You must be humanely treated at all times.

Reprisals against you are not permitted. You cannot be punished for what somebody else has done.

You must be protected against insult or acts of violence by enemy military or civilians.

If you are wounded or sick, you are entitled to the same medical care as a member of the enemy's Army.

The enemy must clothe, feed, and shelter you.

You are a prisoner of war, not a criminal.

195. Genève Pont du Mont Blanc, et Mt. Blanc

Back of this postcard dated October 1944, S/Sgt. Dalrymple wrote: *"The snow-capped mountain is in France. We use to look out of our window and wish we were at the foot of it"*.
(RR)

Dubendorf airfield was the most popular port of call. Busiest day of all was March 18th 1944, when no less than 11 bombers landed.

Switzerland kept strictly to its neutrality and so all aircrew were interned until the end of the war, whether they be British, American or German. Switzerland therefore hosted 1.740 US internees. Many of them tried to escape, these who failed were sent to Wauvilermoos prison camp.

This bill from the Eiger Hotel in Wengen mentioning S/Sgt. Thomas Dalrymple was probably forwarded to the American Legation in Bern to obtain payment. It helps one imagine, even for only two months, the way of life of two airmen internees!

Near Bern, at Munsingen, American servicemen are honoring the memory of their comrades who died in Switzerland. Some crashed, others died from wounds received in flight.
(USAAF)

```
COPY

HOTEL EIGER
    WENGEN
    ---
Telehpon 4526                            6 February 1945
Bahnhofbuffet 4525


Bill for food and drinks charged at the Hotel Eiger Wengen during the
months of August and September 1944 by S/Sgt Dwight Swanson 36366246 and
S/Sgt ......... Dalrymple ........ .

35 whiskeys       at    3.50          122.50
 5 compleats      at    1.00            5.00
 2 suppers        at    3.50            7.00
 1 supper         at    4.00            4.00
 1 bottle wine    at    6.30            6.30
 8 coffees        at     .60            4.80
 8 gin-vermouths  at    1.10            8.80
 5 beers          at     .50            2.50
 1 cider          at     .60             .60
 1 bottle whiskey at   54.00           54.00
                                      ───────
                                      215.50
    10% service                        21.50
                                      237.00

    40.00 franc loan                   40.00
                                      ───────
                                      277.00 Swiss francs

                I certify that the above bill is correct
                and just, and that payment therefor has
                not been received.
                     /s/ fr. Hotel Eiger: EttAnsner

Sgt Swanson and Sgt Dalrymple are AWOL as of September 26, 1944. As
theirs was a joint account I believe they should both be held accountable
for 138.50 swiss francs. We do not have a record of Sgt Dalrymple's first
name or serial number so suggest you check your files for this information.

                    1st Lt. Robert W. Meyer
                    0-672843
                    Commanding Wengen Internment Camp

        Posted 2/27/45
        Wm. P.C.
```

The 12 July 1944 mission.
Target: Munich

Around 1.400 heavy bombers were committed by the 8th AF for this raid, 24 failed to return. 457th BG had 36 planes airborne and bombing was visually made. Visible results appeared to be good. No fighters attacked the formation, but two planes were badly hit by Flak during the bomb run. Each pilot tried to fly to Switzerland. The two planes were serial number 44-6111 and 42-31552.

Serial number 44-6111 was 'Hell's Belle,' piloted by Lt Edward Kozel. It was hit by flak on the bomb run. One engine was knocked off and with other major damage, Kozel decided to reach Switzerland. The plane landed safely at Payerne and the whole crew was interned until the end of the war.

'Hell's Belle' crew was as follows:
Pilot: Lt. Edward Kozel
Copilot: Lt. Alvie J. Phares
Navigator: Lt. Selig Patchick
Bombardier: Lt. Carl F. Altimus
Aircraft engineer: Sg. Robert E. Nichols
Radio operator: Sgt. Jacob L. Alpert
Port waist gunner: Sgt. Dwight F. Sranson
Starboard waist gunner: Sgt. William H. Koester
Tail gunner: S/Sgt. Thomas D. Dalrymple

THE MILITARY ATTACHÉ
LEGATION OF THE
UNITED STATES OF AMERICA
BERN, SWITZERLAND

TO ALL U.S.A.A.F. INTERNEES

Your attention is called once more to standing orders against attempting to escape without my instructions.

Disobedience of these standing orders by a small group of officers and men is bringing about reprisals against the mass of those who are carrying out my orders loyally, thereby creating unnecessary difficulties for this office and serving no useful purpose.

Those who attempt to escape under the present circumstances, in addition to subjecting themselves to such disciplinary action as is deemed appropriate by me, will receive no support from me against punitive action by the Swiss Internment authorities, which will be from 5-6 months' detention at Camp Wauwilermoos.

The present military situation indicates the probability of early repatriation and the wisdom of exercising patience.

29th August 1944

B.R. Legge,
Brigadier General, U.S.A.,
Military Attaché.

Below.
**Dated November 24, 1944, this document mentions the award
of the Air Medal to S/Sgt. Dalrymple while he was interned
in Switzerland.**

GENERAL ORDERS)   R E S T R I C T E D   Hq 1st Bombardment Division
NUMBER   558)   E X T R A C T   APO 557, 24 November 1944.

Under the provisions of Army Regulations 600-45, 22 September 1943, as amended, and pursuant to authority contained in letter, Hq Eighth Air Force, File 200.6, 23 September 1944, subject, "Awards and Decorations", an AIR MEDAL is awarded to the following-named Officers and Enlisted Men, organizations as indicated, Army Air Forces, United States Army.

Citation: For meritorious achievement while participating in sustained bomber combat operations over Germany and German occupied countries. The courage, coolness and skill displayed by these Officers and Enlisted Men upon these occasions reflect great credit upon themselves and the Armed Forces of the United States.

*   *   *   *   *   *

457th Bombardment Group (H)

*   Thomas D. Dalrymple 19180502   S/Sgt Little Rock, Arkansas   *

By command of Brigadier General TURNER:

BARTLETT BEAMAN,
Brigadier General, U. S. Army
Chief of Staff.

OFFICIAL:
ROBERTS P. JOHNSON, JR.,
Lieut. Colonel, A.G.D.,
Adjutant General.

CERTIFIED TRUE COPY: John F. Shinners

JOHN F. SHINNERS
Capt., Air Corps

G

385th Bomb Group

5. 385TH BOMB. GROUP

549TH BOMB. SQUADRON
SGT. IRVIN COURTAD, PHOTOGRAPHER

With four squadrons (548th, 549th, 550th and 551st Bomb. Squadrons), the 385th Bomb. Group was activated in Washington State in December 1942. It was first commanded by Major Elliot Vandevanter (who was later promoted to colonel). The group left for overseas at the beginning of June and was based at Great Ashfield in Suffolk (East Anglia), which became Base 155. The 385th BG accomplished its first mission on July 17th 1943, 28 planes were committed without loss. The most important task at the time for the 8th AF took place on August 17th 1943: the first 'Shuttle' mission to Africa. Targets were the ball bearings plant in Schweinfurt and the aircraft factory in Regensburg in South Germany. For its action on this particular day, the group was awarded a first DUC. Then, the group flew strategic raids over Europe until the end of the war. For its action on May 12th 1944, the 385th BG was awarded a second DUC as it was the leader of the formation during the attack of an aircraft repair plant at Zwickau despite heavy opposition. In June, the unit attacked coastline defenses in preparation for the Normandy invasion. Like other groups of the 8th AF, it was involved in the Normandy campaign to harass enemy troops, and later on during the Battle of the Bulge. In March and April 1945, the group took part in the final offensive. After V-E Day, its B-17s hauled prisoners back from Germany and dropped food in Holland. The 385th returned to the USA in August 1945 where it was inactivated on August 28th. From July 1943 to April 1945, the 385th BG lost 129 planes in action.

Above.
The crew of 'Raunchy Wolf (serial # 42-30249) from 551st Bomb Squadron. She was lost in action on December 30, 1943 on a mission to Ludwigshafen. The plane crashed in France, one crew member was KIA, six became POWs and three evaded capture.
(Courtad)

The 385th Bomb. Group insignia.

Irvin Courtad in issue service coat and garrison cap. He displays a British-made embroidered 8th AF shoulder patch, and a non-regulation USAAF sergeant chevron with the winged propeller motif.
(Courtad)

Aircrew member wings.

The photographic section of the 385th Bomb Group is pictured at Great Ashfield air base in England. Irvin Courtad is standing third from left. Note the aircrew wings of the man seated in front of him.
(Courtad)

Below.
Class booklet of the Lowry Field photographic technical school from which Irvin Courtad was graduated.

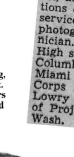

Above.
Photographer specialist sleeve badge, as can be seen on the lower right sleeve of several NCOs on the period picture.

Irvin V. Courtad, son of Mr. and Mrs. W. C. Courtad of 254 Oak street, has been promoted to sergeant at the Army Air base in Great Falls, Mont., where he is stationed with Van's Valiants, a flying fortress group commanded by Lt. Col. Elliott Vandevanter Jr., according to the public relations office there. He entered the service in October and is a group photography laboratory technician. A graduate of St. Mary High school here, he attended the Columbus School of Art and Miami School of Art, the Air Corps School of Photography at Lowry Field, Col., and the School of Projectionists at Geiger Field, Wash.

An ID picture in civilian clothing, included in Courtad's escape kit. These were made to forge papers in case of bail out over Occupied Europe.
(Courtad)

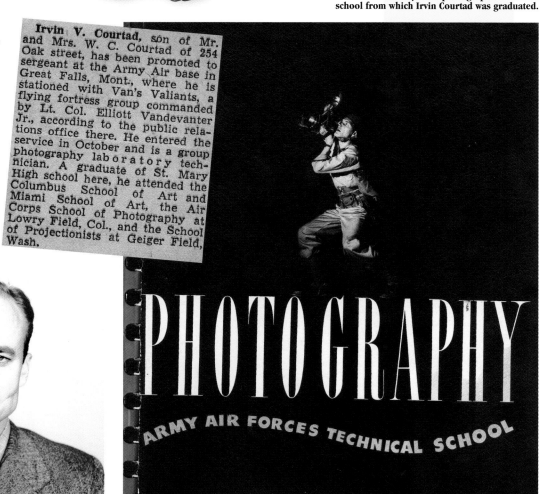

PHOTOGRAPHY

ARMY AIR FORCES TECHNICAL SCHOOL

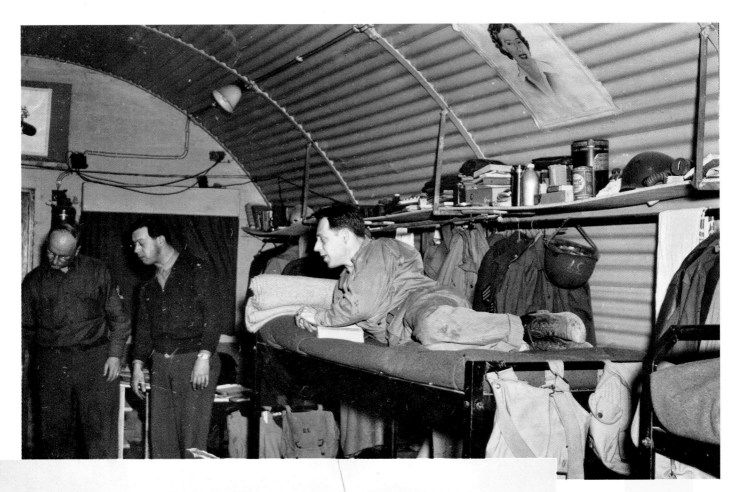

Irvin Courtad at rest
inside a Nissen hut
at Great Ashfield.
(Courtad)

'Lady Susie II' was lost during
the fifth mission of the 385th BG,
on July 29, 1943. She collided
with two other planes, 'Big Stinky'
and 'Round Trip Ticket,' 26 men
were KIA, 4 other became POWs.
(Courtad)

This B-17F was lost on August 17, 1943
during the famous raid over Regensburg
in South Germany, the first 'shuttle'
mission for 8th AF bombers,
which landed in North Africa.
Due to Flak damage, lieutenant Keely
was forced to ditch
on the quiet Mediterranean sea.
The entire crew was saved
by an Air Sea Rescue boat
after spending the night
in dinghies.
(Courtad)

Above.
'Shack Bunny' was shot down by fighters and crashed in Germany on December 13th 1943 during a mission over Kiel.
One crew member was KIA, the nine others became 'Kriegies.'
(Courtad)

Right.
On October 12th 1943, a navigator and a bombardier are about to board their plane. Note the Aviator's Kit Bag used to carry flying gear, and the M1 helmet shell worn over the soft headgear against shell fragments. The navigator is wearing a B-8 back type parachute, the bombardier a QAC harness (Quick Attachable Chest) AN-6513-1A. Both are wearing A-4 flying suits and non-modified A-6 flying boots.
(Courtad)

Below. 'Mary Ellen II' (serial # 42-30601) crash-landed in England on September 16, 1943 after from a mission over Cognac, France.
(Courtad)

September 6, 1944: lieutenant Lamping and crew are posing in front of their plane, 'War Horse.' Note that four crewmen are wearing green A-3 parachute harnesses. This plane crash-landed on November 10, 1944 during a training flight.
(Courtad)

'Hesitatin Hussy' was lost on September 3, 1943. Fully loaded for a mission, the plane caught fire and exploded, badly damaging its hangar. Several nearby B-17s were destroyed and the day's mission was scrubbed.
(Courtad)

'Roundtrip Jack' was lost in September 1944 after a ground accident and was used for spares.
(Courtad)

Perfect view of a B-17F
from the 385th BG during a mission.
Exhaust smudges can be seen
on the wings and engines,
as well as most machine guns.
The red outlined wing cockade
indicates that the photo
was taken between August
and October 1943.
The white square including a G
is the ID marking of the 385th BG
within the 3rd Bomb. division.
(Courtad)

Left.
Lieutenant Louis Dentoni was chief bombardier
of the 385th BG, he was killed in action
in March 1944. Thanks to his ability during
the raid over the Marienburg aircraft works
on October 9th 1943, Air Forces General
Henry H. Arnold described the mission
as the most perfect example
of precision bombing.
(Courtad)

'Winnie The Pooh'
was photographed on August 21,
1943 at Great Ashfield airbase.
This B-17 was lost during a raid
over Regensburg. Shot down
by fighters, she crashed
in Germany. One crew member
was killed, the nine others were
taken prisoner.
(Courtad)

(GPR-20-8-385) (19-8-43) UNDRESSING AFTE

("OHIO AIR FORCE" GUNNERS)

Above.
After a mission, two of of 'Ohio Air Force's' gunners are examining the top turret of their plane (see also page 77). The man on the left is wearing the type F-1 heated flight suit ('Blue Bunny Suit') together with an A-2 jacket. The rest of his equipment is composed of a pair of unaltered A-6 boots, a B-1 cap, a B-4 life jacket and the AN-6513-1A chest type parachute harness.
(Courtad)

Sleepytime Girl

(GPR-24-7-385)(21-8-43)(B

Above and right.
January 12, 1944, 'Sleepytime Girl' and 'Mission Belle' on Great Ashield base. 'Sleepytime Girl' was lost on April 24, 1944 on the way back from a raid over Friedrichschafen. The plane ditched in the Channel. Six crewmen were killed, one captured, the other three evaded capture. 'Mission Belle' was hit on April 11, 1944 during a mission over Politz with lieutenant Pangle's crew. They reached neutral Sweden where all were interned until the end of the war.
(Courtad)

Mission Belle

(GPR-24-11-385)(21-8-43)(B-17 NOSE)

December 16, 1943.
Lieutenant Banks after
a mission over Bremen,
for which the 385th BG
suffered no loss.
Behind him stands
one of the first B-17Gs
delivered to the group,
with its chin turret.
This was lieutenant Banks' 25th
and last mission
before rotating home.
(Courtad)

(16-12-43)(YLT. D.H. BANKS - 25ᵀᴴ MISSION

B-17 PILOT, DECEMBER 1943

December 16, 1943, this B-17 pilot has safely
landed his plane after a dangerous mission
over Kiel harbor in Northern Germany.
He sports a soft officer cap,
that could be worn with headphones,
and a B-3 shearling jacket slipped over a modified A-4
flying suit. His lined boots are unmodified A-6s
and his gloves the A-10 issue. Over the B-3 life vest
he stills has the chest-type RAF parachute harness,
which was often preferred on account
of its quick-release box. This clever and safer device
was not incorporated in airforce chutes until 1944.
The officer also carries a Navigator's leather chart
and instrument case, a leather-covered flak helmet
and an A-8B oxygen mask, the parachute chest pack,
an M-1936 musette bag and ANB-H1 earphones
on a flexible head-band.
(Reconstruction, photo Militaria Magazine)
(Continued on page 74)

Chest-type RAF
parachute harness
and pack.

A B-3 shearling flying jacket and its tag.

TYPE B-3
WG. NO. 33 H 5595
ORDER NO. 42-22898-P
PROPERTY
IR FORCE, U.S. ARM
ERO LEATHER CLO. CO.
EACON, N.Y.
38

Opposite page, top.
Tired, but glad to be alive, this crew of the 551st BS is leaving his B-17G after the first massive raid of the 8th AF over Berlin, in which 810 heavy American bombers were committed. Note the use of the Aviator's Kit Bag to carry flight gear. With 24 planes, the 385th BG was to lead the 3rd bombardment division, totalizing 252 B-17s. This was also the first time the group used the H2-X radar for bombing through overcast. But the Luftwaffe, which had been surprised and disoriented during the two earlier raids, was rarin' for a fight on March 6th 1944. Constant attacks on the way in and back, combined with dense and accurate Flak over Berlin caused the loss of 69 bombers. These were the 8th AF's heaviest losses in a single day of the whole war.
(Courtad)

Bottom left.
Just after the mission over Berlin, a crew member wearing a F–2 heated suit turns in his escape kit. The initial F is for 'France' (see also p. 150). Kneeling, two gunners are inspecting .50 cal. machinegun barrels, which were systematically removed from planes for maintenance and stored in the gun shop until the next flight. The man on the left is only clad in a blue F-1 electrically heated suit. This suit was normally worn as underwear, but this was also currently observed. His neighbor has donned the same suit under heavier clothes. The electrical cables are clearly visible. They are all wearing non-modified A-6 boots.
(Courtad)

Above.
'Sack Time' came to grief on August 17, 1943 during the Regensburg raid. Lieutenant Reichardt's crew was captured after his plane had been shot down by fighters.
(Courtad)

(5-3-44)(BACK FROM BERLIN

PR-183-T-385)(6-3-44)(BACK FROM BERLIN)

**March 6th 1944,
after the Berlin raid,
an Intelligence officer
is interrogating a crew
in order to gather information
on what they observed
during the flight.**
(Courtad)

(GPR-183-5-385)/6-3-44)/ BACK FROM BERLIN)

Abov.
**The USAAF insignia are painted on both lower surfaces
of this P-47 for better identification.
Such markings are typical of 1943.**
(Courtad)

Below.
**November 4, 1943, Major Richard's crew is posing
in front of their own 'Belle of the Blue'
(serial # 42-30094). She survived
the war and flew back to the USA after VE-day.**
(Courtad)

B-17F 'Ohio Air Force'
(serial # 42-30737)
385th BG/549th
BS - January 1944.
(Computer graphics by Nicolas Gohin)

A P-47C escort fighter
of the 8th AF. Bomber crews
nicknamed
them 'little friends'
and their presence was always
felt as very comforting.
(Courtad)

Right.
January 12th 1944.
Lieutenants Richey
and Helman were pictured
with two ground crew before
their B-17 named 'Ohio Air
Force.' Note the number of
kills symbolized
by the swastikas.
'Ohio Air Force' was shot
down by enemy fighters
over France on March 16th
1944 with another crew.
Two were killed,
eight taken prisoner.
(Courtad)

Left.
'Slo Jo' (serial #42-30168)
ditched in the North
Sea on December 11th 1943
with lieutenant Jennings'
crew on board.
Seven men were killed,
the remaining three
were captured.
(Courtad)

Below.
'Mary Pat' (serial #42-3292)
survived the war and returned
to USA in June 1945.
(Courtad)

Ground crew
of 'Belle of the Blue'
are checking one
of her engines.
(Courtad)

'The Dorsal Queen'
(serial #42-0264) was written
off on September 26th 1943
back from a raid over Rheime
with lieutenant Yanello's crew
on board. The whole crew
was killed when the plane
crash landed.
(Courtad)

October 21, 1943, sergeant Simonick is ready to board. Due to persistent fog, that day's mission was canceled. Simonick was assigned to captain Binks' crew in the 550th BS. Note the unusual cockade insignia with underlined star and blurred outline. The NCO wears a fur-lined B-6 helmet modified with earcups and ANB-H1 earphones, and a B-3 life jacket over his A-2 flying jacket.
(Courtad)

(21-10-43)(S/SGT. J. S. SIMONICK · 550 SQ.)

Left.
An all-girl band is rehearsing before a party on the 385th BG base.
(Courtad)

Left.
'Roundtrip Ticket II' (serial #42-30414) was salvaged for spares in August 1944.
(Courtad)

Below.
'Piccadilly Queen' (serial #42-30251) crashed in Germany after a mid-air collision with another plane. Six crew members were killed, the four other were taken prisoner.
(Courtad)

October 19, 1943, S/Sgt. R. Palmer emerges from his ball turret. Research in the 385th BG archives indicate that Palmer was not assigned to a particular crew.
(Courtad)

Right.
'Fickle Finger of?' (serial #42-3335) survived the war but was scrapped in England before the 385th BG flew home.
(Courtad)

Above.
In North Africa on the outbound leg of a shuttle mission, local children are posing with crew members around a souvenir which they are about to bring back in England.
(Courtad)

Top right.
The same trophy – apparently part of a Ju-87 Stuka – exhibited at Great Ashfield airbase, after being flown back from North Africa by 385 BG crews who had taken part in the Regensburg raid on 17 August 1943.
(Courtad)

Right.
January 1944, Major Ross was pictured in the nose of a B-17 manning a .50 cal. machine gun and with an ammunition belt around the neck.
(Courtad)

Right.
**This B-17F named 'Nan B'
(serial # 42-3355) is pictured
during a mission towards
the end of summer 1943.
As the ball turret machine guns
are pointing down, the gunner
has not climbed down yet.**
(Courtad)

Below.
**April 28th 1944, after landing
back from a mission over
Cherbourg (France), lieutenant
Anderson is seated at the
navigator's table
in the nose of a B-17.**
(Courtad)

B-17F 'Nan B' (serial # 42-3355)
385th BG/550th BS - July 1943.
(Computer graphics by Nicolas Gohin)

Right.
January 6, 1944, lieutenants W.C. Gregg and J.E. Richey are congratulating each other for the Distinguished Flying Cross (DFC) they have just been awarded.
(Courtad)

Below.
The original 550th BS insignia, which was changed in 1944.

The new 550th BS insignia, which replaced the hedgehog in 1944.

Left.
The 385th BG officers' club decorated with pilot wings, the group insignia and the four squadrons.' Far right, the 550th BS insignia is still the older pattern.
(Courtad)

October 6th 1943, lieutenant Whitlow's crewmen are posing in front of their plane in England. Four days later, on a mission over Munster, their B-17 (serial# 42-3539) was shot down by German fighters over Holland. Three of them were killed in action, four were taken prisoner and three managed to reach England.
(Courtad)

(6-10-43

LT. W.B. WHITLOW'S CREW #18 - 549TH

Above.
**The 549th Bomb. Squadron
insignia.**

Left.
**This officer is probably
Major Archie Benner,
the 549th Bomb Squadron
commander, he wears
its insignia on his
A-2 jacket.**
(Courtad)

Below.
**July 28th 1943, despite Flak damage to the starboard tail
elevator, this B-17F named 'Fickle Finger Of', succeeded
in coming back to Great Ashfield airbase. It was the fifth
mission for the 385th BG, the target was Oscherleben.**
(Courtad)

Bottom left.
**Captain Witherspoon was pictured in a bright mood
in the cockpit of his B-17 on October 8, 1943
just before a mission to Bremen.**
(Courtad)

Opposite page, far right.
**After a mission, aviators and ground
crews are gathering around an American
Red Cross 'doughnut wagon.'**
(Courtad)

B-17G 'Lil Audrey'
(serial # 42-32008)
385th BG/551st BS -
July 1944.
*(Computer graphics
by Nicolas Gohin)*

LiL AUDREY

Bombs bays open, these planes of the 385th BG are dropping their bombs, as a Flak shell is exploding near the first B-17G named 'Lil Audrey' (serial # 42-32008). This plane survived the war and returned home.
(Courtad)

Left.
In the radio compartment of a B-17, through a special port, this photographer is ready to take aerial shots. Note the uncommon A-9 oxygen mask, identified by its 'brow' strap, oddly worn under the B-6 flying helmet and a pair of earphones.
(Courtad)

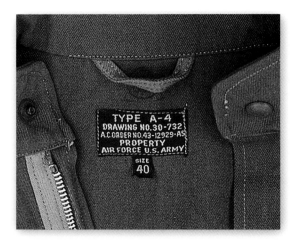

Right.
The flying suit tag. In the USAAF equipment nomenclature, A-5 stands for an improvement of the A-4 pattern. The A-4 indeed received zippers to close chest and thigh pockets so loose items and survival kits would not be lost when bailing out of the plane. The new type was not included in manufacturer's tags, however, and this suit made in 1943 is still catalogued as an A-4.

Left and above.
The K-20 portable camera. Many shots of USAAF airbases were also taken with this camera. It was however mostly carried in some bombers within the formation to take pictures from the waist gunners' positions amidship, especially snapshots of bomb patterns on the ground. By comparing these shots with those taken previously by photo reconnaissance planes, the intelligence analysts could rate the accuracy and effectiveness of the bombing. The right-hand side handle also acts as cocking lever, the trigger on top activates the shutter. The back part accommodates the film plates, in 4 x 5 inch format. The sight on top is retractable. This particular camera was manufactured in 1942 by the Folmer Graflex Corporation, Rochester, New York.

Below, left.
Standard A-6 flying boots. These were later modified with a strap on the instep so they would not come off when the parachute canopy unfurled.

Bottom.
The A-6 boots manufacturer's tag mentions an AC (Air Corps, before it became the USAAF) contract No and Bristolite, the manufacturer. Other boots were made by Converse or U.S. Rubber Co.

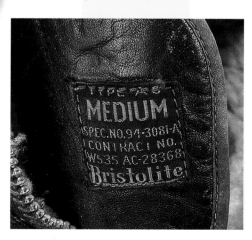

90

AERIAL PHOTOGRAPHER, JULY 1943

This aerial photographer has just stepped down from his B–17 F after a raid.
With his K-20 camera, he finishes off the remaining film
by shooting stills of his shipmates near their plane.
His flying gear is made of an A-5 flying suit, a B-6 life jacket, an A-2 flying jacket, a pair
of A-10 gloves and a B-6 helmet altered with added earcups for R-14 earphones.
His goggles are the B-7 type, the oxygen mask is an A-9. He has the harness for the AN-6513-1A
chest-pack chute. After all heavy gear had been collected and packed in bags,
escape kits were returned to the pilot and personnel boarded
a 6x6 truck bound for the locker room.
(Reconstruction, photo Militaria Magazine)

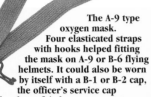

The A-9 type
oxygen mask.
Four elasticated straps
with hooks helped fitting
the mask on A-9 or B-6 flying
helmets. It could also be worn
by itself with a B-1 or B-2 cap,
the officer's service cap
or garrison cap, thanks to a headnet of 4 short straps
and hooks that can be seen here.

Below.
Three photographers are boarding a B-17 for a mission,
their job will be to record visual information for the group's
intelligence officers. Note the transport case
for the Kodak type K-20 camera.
(Courtad)

As this photo shows,
helmets and Flak jackets were
sometimes flimsy protection
against heavy shell fragments.
(Courtad)

Above.
This shot was taken during one of the first missions
of the 385th BG early in July 1943. The first plane showing
a nude woman and the monicker 'Sack Time' was lost
on August 17th 1943 during the raid over Regensburg.
The ten members of lieutenant Reichardt's crew succeeded
in bailing out, but all were taken prisoner.
(Courtad)

Below.
Colonel Vandevanter
is congratulating
a subordinate. The 385th
CO dresses like a British
officer, with swagger stick,
overseas cap and fine
leather gloves.
(Courtad)

Below.
February 1st 1944, colonel Vandevanter and Major Lewis are
pictured while celebrating the group's first year in England.
(Courtad)

Above.

Inside a B-17, this photographer handling a Kodak type K-20 camera is pictured at a waist gunner's station. The lack of oxygen mask and the unconnected belt of ammo suggest that this shot was taken on the homeward leg of a mission, near the English coast.

(Courtad)

Right.

This aerial photographer is posing in full flight gear in front of a hut at Great Ashfield base. His flight gear is composed of a type A-4 flight suit, a type B-4 life jacket, type A-6 non-modified boots, a type B-6 modified leather flying helmet, AN-6530 goggles, and a Quick Attachable Chest (QAC) AN-6513-1A chute harness. Note the control tag on the chest pack.

(Courtad)

Corporal Ruby Newell from Long Beach, California, was elected prettiest WAC in the ETO after a *Stars and Stripes* contest. This studio portrait was used by Corp. Closs to paint the nose art of 'Ruby's Raiders' at right.
(Courtad)

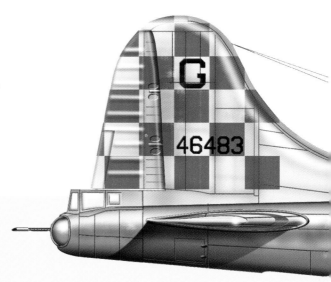

Below.
July 30, 1944, at the port waist gun position of a B-17, S/Sgt Parker pretends to repel a fighter attack. On his right, against the fuselage, the portable oxygen tank could explode if hit.
(Courtad)

(30-7-44)(S/SGT. G.W. PARKER)

This picture was taken at the plane commissioning ceremony when the crew met Ruby Newell.
(Courtad)

The M3
Flak helmet.

The british-issue
Wilkinson
Flak vest was
frequently worn
by 8th Air Force crews.

Because of bad weather, no mission
was flown on May 16th 1944. Lieutenant
Engle's crew seized the opportunity
to be pictured in front of its B-17G.
The four kneeling officers are wearing QAC
AN-6513-1A chest type parachute harnesses.
The other crew members,
except for the 2nd man from the right,
have type A-3 harnesses. A gunner, far right,
has penned his wife or girlfriend's name
under the bill of his cap.
The second and third airmen from the right
have A-3 HBT caps, normally issued to
ground crews.
(Courtad)

(GO-19-1-385)(19-44)(M-4) INCEN.

500 LB.
M76

LOT 3
INCENDIARY

P -44

0.1 CU. FT.

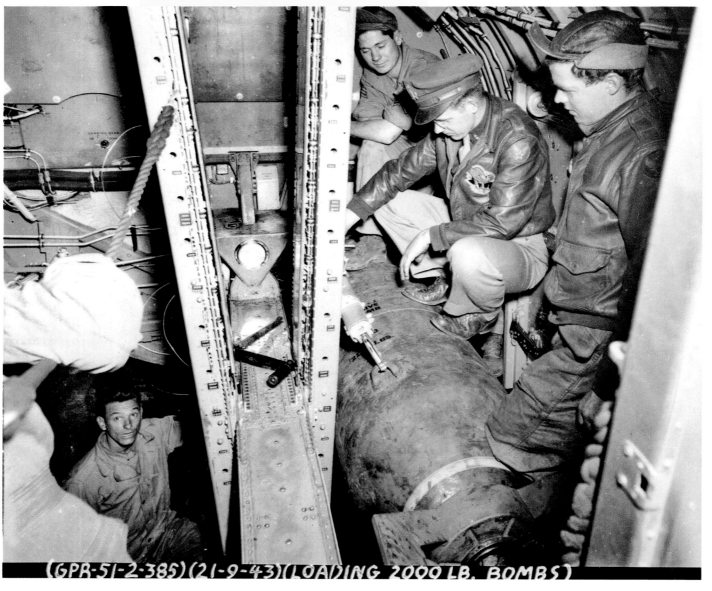

(GPR-51-2-385)(21-9-43)(LOADING 2000 LB. BOMBS)

Previous page, top.
**The incendiary bomb dump on Great Ashfield base.
Two armorers are fusing M-47 incendiary bombs.**
(Courtad)

Left.
**Different types of incendiary bombs loaded into 8th AF
bombers. From left to right: the M-76 bomb filled
with jellied gasoline, magnesium powder and sodium nitrate,
the M-17 aimable cluster containing 110 M-50A1 magnesium
incendiaries, and the 100-lb M-47A2 napalm-filled bomb.**
(Courtad)

Previous page, bottom.
**September 21, 1943. Crewmen of the 549th Bomb Squadron
load a 2.000-lb in the bomb bay of a B-17.**
(Courtad)

Right and bottom, right.
**March 15, 1944, back from a mission
over Brunswick, the B–17G
'Honky Tonk Sal' (serial# 42-31335)
succeeded in limping back to Great
Ashfield although badly damaged.
Crewmen and ground personnel
are trying to free the tail gunner from
his compartment, crushed
under the collapsed tailfin.
It was a common occurrence for battered
US bombers to fly back to England
'on a wing and a prayer.'**
(Courtad)

Above.
**Wounded but alive,
this gunner is lifted
from his plane
to an ambulance.**
(Courtad)

Top, left.
June 6th 1944: this photo was taken just
the 385th BG's first mission of the day. Col. Vandevanter
is photographed with lieutenants Batty, Berry and Jones.
They are wearing light A-4 or ANS-31a flying suits,
except Lt. Jones who has a B-10 jacket.
(Courtad)

Above.
Approaching a cloud layer, a formation of planes
from the 385th BG is dropping its bombs.
(Courtad)

Left.
A bombardier in the nose of a B-17F. He wears issue wool
trousers, an A-2 leather flying jacket
and unaltered A-6 lined boots.
(Courtad)

Opposite page, bottom.
Lieutenant Mudge's crew from the 549th Bomb Squadron
in front of their plane 'Hustlin Hussy' (serial # 42-30354)
on November 4, 1943. She was shot down by German fighters
on January 29th 1944 and crashed in Belgium.
Most of the crew evaded capture, one was killed,
two others were taken prisoner.
(Courtad)

Above.
Irvin Courtad's bicycle registration card.

Right.
The airbase bicycle repair shop. Bicycles were indispensable to run short errands on the field and were helping to save on gas.
(Courtad)

Lieutenant Salyard's crew from the 550th Bomb Squadron was pictured in England on February 20th 1944. Their plane was shot down by Flak on a mission over Brunswick on March 23rd 1944. All bailed out safely but were captured.
(Courtad)

(10-5-44) (T/Sgt G G CROFT)

(22-11-43) (LT. MUDGE'S CREW - 549 SQD)

B-17G 'Sky Chief
(serial # 42-32008)
385th BG/548th BS -
March 1944.
(Computer graphics by Nicolas Gobin)

Below.
'Sky Chief' was a B-17G
(serial # 42-39912) flown
by lieutenant Courcel.
It was written off on July 16th
1944 after a crash landing
in England. The crew
on the photo is not identified.
(Courtad)

Inset.
A B-17 radio operator in his compartment.
(Courtad)

Above.
A B-17G over occupied Europe.
Yellow stripes around the fuselage indicate
a radio relay aircraft for the wing.
(Courtad)

LIEUTENANT MARYONOVICH'S ODYSSEY

Lieutenant Maryonovich was photographed
in England on February 18, 1944 after a long epic which
started during a mission over Bordeaux (France).
His B-17 named 'Suzanne' (serial # 42-3294) came down
in the sea near Portugal just after escaping German fighters
by diving through the clouds. With two engines out,
decision had been made to try and reach Spain and follow
the coast until Gibraltar. But both the weather and lack
of gas made Lisbon their final destination. In order to wreck
the bomber, Maryonovich ditched it in Lisbon Bay.
The ship stayed afloat for 20 minutes, the crew fired flares
and a fishing boat picked them up an hour later.
They were brought to the village of Czembra for a warm
welcome. The British Consul arrived about midnight
and drove them back to Lisbon where they were turned over
to the American attaché. The Hotel de San Antonio became
their home for the next seven days. New passports were made
with the photos in their escape kits. They were fitted
with civilian clothing but had to retain their GI boots.
They went sightseeing in Lisbon and one night, boarded
a ship back to Ireland, and then to London for a debriefing.
Somebody had decided they were not escapees or internees,
but merely 'shipwrecked mariners' in international waters.
For these reasons, their operational tour was deemed
to be over.
(Courtad)

Above and above, left.
August 23rd 1944, colonel Vandevanter is about to pass his command in review for the last time prior to his leaving the 385th BG. He is chatting with Brigadier General A.W. Kissner, 3rd Bombardment Division chief of staff, while the new commanding officer, col. George Y. Jumper (from the 447th BG, pictured above) and the wing commander, Brigadier General Castle, look on.
(Courtad)

Left and below.
These two shots were taken on September 30th 1944 during the 200th Mission Party. British civilians, servicemen and women, were guests of the Americans at Great Ashfield. More than 1,500 girls were hosted, 200 of them coming from London by special train. Major Glenn Miller's 50-musician band performed in a hangar and, through the efforts of the BBC, a part of the program was broadcast to the States.
(Courtad)

105

Above.
'Dorsal Queen' (serial #42-30822) was lieutenant Gray's ship. Less than a month after this shot was taken, on February 25, she was shot down by Flak and crashed in Germany.
(Courtad)

Below.
Back from a mission, these crew members are enjoying a hot drink and some doughnuts.
(Courtad)

This strange machine created and used by the 385th BG was indeed a training device for bombardiers, as well as a tool for adjusting Norden bombsights.
(Courtad)

Above.
**A radio operator at his MG station. This gun was deleted on later variants
of the B-17. Note that the barrel has been removed to be cleaned and stored until
the next flight in the armament shop.**
(Courtad)

Below.
**Early in the morning of May 23, 1944, an enemy airplane dropped seven bombs
on the Great Ashfield base. One hit hangar No. 1 and destroyed B-17 'Powerful Katrina.'
Disregarding the cooked-off .50 ammo and the explosion hazard, firemen went right in
and fought the fire until it was extinguished, thus saving another ship nearby.
Intrusions by elite Luftwaffe pilots were a permanent threat. A single fighter marauding
in the landing circuit was always feared.**
(Courtad)

Above.
**Captain Gerald Binks was the 550th BS operations officer.
He was killed on February 23rd 1944 during a raid over
Diepholz when his plane collided with another in the same
formation.**
(Courtad)

Above.
Near the B-17's 'tail sting,' these two gunners are posing for the photographer. The airman in leather jacket has ground troops' leather and wool gloves.
(Courtad)

Right.
A waist gunner at his position. He is wearing an RAF type B helmet.
(Courtad)

Below.
B-17G 'Wells Cargo' lost its hydraulics and made an emergency landing at Great Ashfield. The ship was repaired and ended the war.
(Courtad)

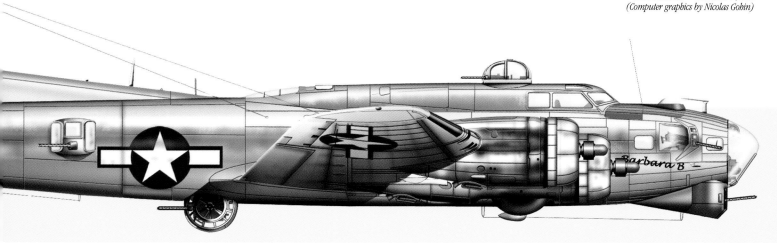

B-17G 'Barbara B'
(serial # 42-32078) 385th
BG/550th BS - October 1944.
(Computer graphics by Nicolas Gohin)

Above.
Framed by Flak explosions, 'Barbara B' (serial # 42-32078) is dropping its load simultaneously with other planes in the formation. This B-17G ended the war unscathed and returned to the USA in June 1945. Note the M-17 cluster straight below the bomb bay: this metal cylinder scattered magnesium incendiaries at a preset altitude for optimal target coverage.
(Courtad)

Right.
February 15, 1944, captain W.C. Gregg (see also p. 85) is pictured with his copilot in the cockpit of a B-17. No mission was flown by the group between February 13th and 20th.
(Courtad)

6. 447TH BOMB. GROUP

**708TH BOMB. SQUADRON
2ND LT. ALLEN J. MILLER, NAVIGATOR
30 MISSIONS**

The 447th Bombardment Group was established on April 6th 1943 with four squadrons (708th, 709th, 710th, 711th bomb. squadrons). It trained with B-17s, its first CO was colonel Hunter Harris Jr. from May 23, 1943 to September 24, 1944.

The unit moved to England in November 1943 and was based at Rattlesden (USAAF station # 126) until August 1945. Combat missions started in December 1943 and until May 1944, the group helped to prepare for the Invasion by attacking submarine bases, cities in Germany, ports and V-weapons sites in France, airfields and marshalling yards in France, Belgium, and Germany.

At the end of February 1944, the unit took part in the intensive campaign against the German aircraft industry. It supported the Normandy landings in June 1944 by bombing airfields and other targets near the beachhead. The group flew tactical missions at Saint-Lô in July and in the effort

Above.
**Allen Miller's sterling
silver Navigator wings.**

Top.
**2nd Lieutenant Allen Miller
is ready to board the plane
and sit at his navigation table.
He's wearing an AN-J-4
fur-lined jacket, a B-4 life
jacket and an A-3 parachute
harness.**
(USAAF)

to seize Brest in September. Its planes also dropped supplies to the French resistance during the summer of 1944.

The group bombed enemy positions to assist the airborne endeavor in Holland in September. On September 25th 1944, colonel Harris was replaced by col. William Wrigglesworth. From October to December 1944, the 447th BG struck oil production plants in Germany.

2nd Lt. Robert Femoyer (navigator) was awarded the Medal of Honor for his action on November 2nd 1944. During a mission over Germany, his B-17 was badly damaged by Flak and Femoyer was severely wounded by shell fragments. He succeeded in navigating the plane out of danger and saved the crew. Refusing a sedative shot, for more than two hours he steered the bomber home without further damage. Lt. Femoyer died shortly after being removed from the plane.

During the Battle of the Bulge (December 1944-January 1945) the group hit marshalling yards, railroad bridges and communication hubs in the combat zone.

Then the 447th BG resumed operations against strategic targets in Germany, raiding synthetic oil plants, oil storage areas, transportation and communications networks, and many other objectives until the war ended. During this period, the group also supported the airborne assault across the Rhine in March 1945.

On March 31st Lt-colonel Louis G. Thorup replaced colonel Wrigglesworth and led the group until the end of the war. The 447th returned to the US in August 1945 and was inactivated on November 7, 1945.

From December 1943 to April 1945, on 247 missions, the 447th BG lost 97 B-17s in action.

Right .
At Ellington Field in Texas, cadets of class 43-20N are posing in front of their barracks.
(USAAF)

Bottom.

Allen Miller's awards during his operational tour in Europe, from left to right:
— Distinguished Flying Cross,
— Air Medal with 3 Oak Leaf Cluster devices (for 3 additional awards),
— European Campaign Medal with 4 battle stars,
— American Campaign Medal
— Victory Medal.

Below.
The cadets' mess at San Marcos Navigation school.
On the menu: hamburgers and Falstaff beer for everyone.
(USAAF)

Below.
Class 43-20 booklet with which Miller was graduated. This class was mixed, with both navigator and bombardier trainees.

Left.
Crew n° 157-17.
Standing from left to right:
Jerome Farey (radio),
Allen Miller (navigator),
James Liakos (bombardier),
Lyndon Lakeman (co-pilot),
Dale Hanks (pilot).
Kneeling from left to right:
Richard Carne (ball turret
gunner), John Comeau
(tail gunner), Grady Hawk
(waist gunner),
Vincent Bartilucci
(flight engineer),
Inocencio Vargas
(waist gunner).
(USAAF)

Below.
Lieutenant Lyndon Lakeman (copilot in lt. Hank's ship)
is pictured with his mother at Manchester (New Hampshire)
before leaving the USA.
(RR)

Below.
Lieutenant Miller's
Physical record card.

INSTRUCTIONS

1. This form will be carried by all rated officers on flying status and all enlisted crew members on flying status.

2. Record will be initiated and maintained by Flight Surgeons.

3. Form will be submitted for inspection to Flight Surgeon, Operations Officer and/or other interested persons upon request.

4. New form will be prepared by Flight Surgeon when indicated or required.

5. This form is for use in the Army Air Forces to supplement W. D., A. G. O. Form No. 64.

6. A. A. F. Regulation No. 15-206 governs use and procurement of this form.

16-41368-1

ARMY AIR FORCES
AIR CREW MEMBER
PHYSICAL RECORD CARD

W. D., A. A. F. FORM NO. 206
Revised 14 Sept. 1944

Dated March 30, 1944, these movement orders indicate that lieutenant Hanks' crew
(including Miller as navigator) is assigned overseas on the B-17 serial # 42-107071.
They are relieved from training, and are ordered to reach Presque Isle (Maine)
by military plane, the first leg of the transcontinental flight.

R E S T R I C T E D

HEADQUARTERS KEARNEY ARMY AIR FIELD
Kearney, Nebraska

370.5-344 (157-17)

SUBJECT: Movement Orders, Heavy Bombardment Crew Number FZ-400-AJ-17, To Overseas Destination.   30 March 1944

TO:

P	2nd Lt	DALE J HANKS	
CP	2nd Lt	LYNDON F LAKEMAN	0810874
N	2nd Lt	ALLEN J MILLER	0818887
B	2nd Lt	JAMES L LIAKOS	0707087
E	Sgt	Vincent D Bartilucci	0757727
R	Sgt	Jerome R Farey	32790625
AG	Sgt	John M Comeau	32732940
CG	Cpl	Richard F Carne	32719686
CG	Sgt	Grady L Hawk	16083905
CG	Sgt	Inocencio A Vargas	34587225
			39294938

1. You are assigned to Shipment FZ-400-AJ, as crew No. FZ-400-AJ-17, and to B-17 airplane number 42-107071, on aircraft project number 92644-R. You are equipped in accordance with the provisions of the movement order.

2. You are relieved from atchd unasgnd 271st Army Air Force Base Unit (SP), this station, and WP via mil acft and/or rail to AAB, Presque Isle, Maine, or such other Air Port of Embarkation as the CG, ATC, may direct, thence to the overseas destination of Shipment FZ-400-AJ. Upon arrival at the Air Port of Embarkation, control of the above personnel is relinquished to the CG, ATC.

3. This is a PERMANENT change of station. You will not be accompanied by dependents; neither will you be joined by dependents enroute to, nor at, the Air Port of Embarkation. You will not discuss this movement except as may

Right.
April 29, 1944:
shortly before taking off
for a mission to Berlin.
Refuelling is underway,
the crew is ready to board
the B-17 'Butch II.'
The ship already boasts seven
enemy fighter kills,
while flown by its former crew.
This was to be Allen Miller's
second flight.
(USAAF)

Below.
By order of the USAAF
Headquarters dated April 8,
1944, Miller's crew is assigned
to the 708th Bomb. Squadron
of the 8th Air Force.

SPECIAL ORDERS)	HEADQUARTERS
:	USAAF STA 126, APO 559
NUMBER 95)	18 Apr '44

1. Having rptd this Sta per par 1, Sec I, SO #105, Hq, 8th AFRD, 15 Apr '44, the
following Off, AC, and EM are asgd to orgns indicated.

Asgd to 708th Bomb Sq (H)		Asgd to 709th Bomb Sq (H)	
(P) 2D LT DALE J. HANKS	0810874	(P) 2D LT FRANKLIN R. CHAIMSON	0689944
(CP) 2D LT LYNDON F. LAKEMAN	0818887	(CP) 2D LT CRAIG T. KELLOGG	0818880
(N) 2D LT ALLEN J. MILLER	0707087	(N) 2D LT JOHN S. TOMCIK	0703342
(B) 2D LT JAMES L. LIAKOS	0757727	(B) 2D LT OSCAR (NMI) IEZMAN	0684158
Sgt (748) Vincent D. Bartilucci	32790625	S Sgt (748) Dominick R. Lorusso	32486357
Sgt (612) John M. Comeau	32719686	S Sgt (757) John E. Nunez, Jr.	39557899
Sgt (757) Jerome R. Farey	32732940	Sgt (748) Raymond (NMI) Hindle	11079815
Sgt (612) Inocencio A. Vargas	39294938	Sgt (748) Isaac A. Jackson	13119356
Sgt (748) Grady L. Hawk	34587225	Sgt (612) Norman H. Kirby	38425634
Cpl (611) Richard F. Carne	16083905	Sgt (611) James J. Stamas	16137722

Below.
After a mission,
these crew members
are boarding a GMC truck bound
for the locker rooms.
The man in the middle
is holding a navigation map
including photos of the target.
Far right, another airman
has already taken
off his electrically-heated
jacket and is wearing a towel
around the neck to mop sweat.
Far left, an officer with
a B-8 back type parachute holds
an M1 steel helmet to protect
against Flak fragments.
(USAAF)

LIEUTENANT MILLER'S THIRTY MISSIONS

Mission 1.
April 27, 1944 - Louvain, Belgium - duration 6 hrs.
The target was cloud-covered so the planes bombed Le Culot airfield. Flak was heavy resulting in the loss of one B-17 of the 447th BG (Lt. Guynn's crew). Results were fair. Planes returned to base at 21 hrs, requiring a night landing. Escort fighters shot down three enemy fighters in the air and destroyed four on the ground for the loss of 4 P-47s.

Mission 2.
April 29, 1944 - Berlin, Germany - 8 hrs.
Briefing was held at 04.30, 618 heavy bombers were committed. Planes carried incendiary and general purpose HE bombs. The bombing altitude was 22.000 feet. On the way to the target, formation was harassed by enemy fighters, causing several losses.
Over the target, Flak was heavy and more planes were shot down. The 447th BG lost 10 B-17s, the 8th AF 63 planes. Impacts on target were unobserved.

Mission 3.
May 7, 1944 - Berlin, Germany - 9.15 hrs.

Briefing was at 03.30. There was a gasp when crews learned that the target was Berlin. The purpose of the raid was to lure the Luftwaffe into a major fight. The formation left the English coast south of Great Yarmouth and crossed the continent at the bombing altitude (24.000 feet). As usual over Berlin, Flak barrages were accurate and intense, but no enemy aircraft were to be seen. Fighter escort was excellent. The 447th BG suffered no losses. For the first time in history, 1.000 heavy bombers were airborne on a single mission.

Mission 4.
May 8, 1944 - Berlin, Germany - 6 hrs.
Briefing was at 03.30 AM. When the curtain rose before the mission map there was a groan, Berlin again! A part of the formation was separated from the stream and bombed Brunswick, Magdeburg and Brandenburg. Other planes found the target and had an uneventful mission, dropping their bombs through the clouds. Escort fighters claimed 55 enemy fighters for the loss of 13. On the way back over southern England, crews observed men and matériel concentrations in preparation for the landing in Normandy.

MILLER, ALLEN J.   2nd   Lt   O-707087   OPERATIONAL MISSIONS

	DATE		TARGET				
1.	27 Apr 44	6:00	Louvain Adrm	16.	7 June 44	Nantes, Fr.	8:30
2.	29 Apr 44	8:00	Berlin, Ger.	17.	12 June 44	Conches	6:30
3.	7 May 44	9:15	Berlin, Gr.	18.	14 June 44	Florennes	6:30
4.	8 May 44	6:00	Berlin, Ger.	19.	18 June 44	Misburg	8:00
5.	12 May 44	9:00	Zwickau	20.	22 June 44	Micourt	6:30
6.	22 May 44	7:30	Kiel, Ger.	21.	28 June 44	Denain Prouvy	6:30
7.	24 May 44	9:00	Berlin, Ger.	22.	11 July 44	Munich	9:15
8.	25 May 44	6:00	Brussels, Belg.	23.	12 July 44	Munich	9:45
9.	28 May 44	8:00	Konigsborn	24.	18 July 44	Duxhaven	6:30
10.	29 May 44	8:15	Leipzig	25.	21 July 44	Regensburg	9:00
11.	31 May 44	6:30	Hamm, Ger.	26.	11 Aug. 44	Belfort	9:00
12.	2 June 44	4:45	Boulogne	27.	26 Aug. 44	Brest	6:30
13.	3 June 44	5:00	Audeselles	28.	8 Sept 44	Mainz	7:30
14.	6 June 44	6:00	Caen, Fr.	29.	9 Sept 44	Serial A	8:00
15.	6 June 44	6:30	Argentan	30.	10 Sept 44	Giebelstadt	7:30

This chit sums up lt. Miller's 30 combat missions and their characteristics (date, target, flying time) are also told extensively from this page on.

Bombs bay open…
Over target…
Bombs away!
The white plume is coming
from a smoke marker diving towards
the target. The planes seen here
were Pathfinders, being
the first over the target area.
(USAAF)

Mission 5.
May 12, 1944 - Zwickau, Germany - 9 hrs.
Briefing was at 06.00. Clear weather was forecast over Central Germany. The target was an aircraft repair depot. Planes crossed the French coast between Dunkirk and Ostend. There were 700 enemy fighters airborne. The 447th BG hit the target with good results but lost 7 planes during several head-on attacks.

Mission 6.
May 22th, 1944 - Kiel, Germany - 7.30 hrs.
The target was the port area at Kiel. The bomber wave assembled in bad weather, but the planes succeeded in bombing visually with good results and no losses.

Mission 7.
May 24, 1944 - Berlin, Germany - 9 hrs.
27 crews reported to the briefing room at 04.30. Target was Berlin once more. Over the objective, Flak was spotty and inaccurate. During an enemy fighter attack, one plane got caught in the prop wash and the pilot lost control. The craft flipped on its back and plunged to earth in a spin. No aircrew bailed out. Their bodies were washed ashore in the Netherlands.

Mission 8.
May 25, 1944 - Brussels, Belgium - 6 hrs.
The target was the marshalling yards in the southern part of Brussels. Results were rated as excellent. No enemy aircraft was seen, there were no losses.

Mission 9.
May 28, 1944 - Konigsborn, Germany - 8hrs.
The target was an oil depot. The group made a clear weather assembly and left the English coast at Great Yarmouth. The bombing altitude was 24.000 feet. The planes dropped their bombs as the lead planes dropped theirs and returned home with no losses. The force of 864 heavies lost 32 planes.

Mission 10.
May 29, 1944 - Leipzig, Germany - 8.15 hrs.
Reveille for crews at 04.00 AM in the early dawn light. The briefing started at 05.30. The intelligence officer announced that the target was a Me.109 plant in Leipzig. The bombing altitude was reached as the formation crossed the Dutch coast. The weather was clear. Over target the Flak was accurate and very dense. One B-17 of the 447th BG (Lt. Moran's crew) was shot down. The wing ahead was hit by enemy fighters. The 8th AF lost 34 heavy bombers.

Mission 11.
May 31, 1944 - Hamm, Germany - 6.30 hrs.
30 crews attended the briefing at 04.30 AM. The target was the marshalling yards. A bad weather assembly was made and the formation had to change course due to bad weather. But the target was hit with excellent results and no losses.

Mission 12.
June 2, 1944 - Boulogne, France - 4.45 hrs.
Target was a heavy coastal battery north of Boulogne. Assembly was difficult. The weather began to clear over London. PFF plane failed to pick up the target. Group returned to base without losses.

Mission 13.
June 3, 1944 - Audeselles, France - 5 hrs.
Briefing started at 06.00 AM. The target was coastal defenses in the Pas-de-Calais in order to persuade the Germans that the Invasion would come soon in this part of France. Bomb run was satisfactory with no flak and no losses.

Mission 14.
June 6, 1944 - Caen, France - 6 hrs.
Briefing started at 02.00. 45 crews were present as colonel Harris announced that the Invasion was on, the 82nd and 101st Airborne divisions being dropped in the early hours of the morning. The 447th BG had to bomb the area north of Caen. Bu heavy bombers were not effective on D-Dday. Many of them flew back with their bomb load.

Mission 15.
June 6, 1944 - Argentan, France - 6.30 hrs
The third mission of the day was scheduled for 17.50 PM. The target remained the same. Due to the bad weather the PFF radar operator lost the target and no secondary target could be located. The planes returned to base with their bombs. The 8th AF committed 782 heavy bombers, but only 508 actually bombed.

Mission 16.
June 7, 1944 - Nantes, France - 8.30 hrs.
Briefing was at 14.30 PM. Mission was a tactical one over Tours. Take-off started at 17.00. The stream assembled in bad weather. Thousands of ships of all sizes could be observed on the Channel. Crew members could see shells exploding far inland within enemy lines. The primary target was obscured by clouds, so the formation set course for Nantes, the secondary target. The group made a run on a railroad bridge, but did not bomb. Flak was moderate, but accurate. There were 'bandits' lurking near the base so the formation was redirected towards fields in Northwest England. Landings started there at 01.30.

Mission 17.
June 12, 1944 - Conches, France - 6.30 hrs.
Briefing was at 03.00. Target: railroads in Northwest France. The outbound flight was short, but the group missed the IP (Initial Point) and set course for the secondary target, but was unable to locate it. It then switched to a target of opportunity, the Conches airstrip near Paris. Results were quoted as fair. There were no losses.

Mission 18.
June 14, 1944 - Florennes, Belgium - 6.30 hrs.
There were 39 crews present for the briefing at 01.30. The target was the large Luftwaffe airbase at Florennes in Belgium, near the French border. Weather was clear over target, results rated as excellent.

Mission 19.
June 18, 1944 - Misburg, Germany - 8rs.
Briefing was at 02.30. The target was an oil refinery at Misburg. Colonel Harris, the 447th CO, flew in a PFF ship leading the main group. The formation was at 19.000 feet as it crossed the Dutch coast. Flak was heavy over target. Two planes were hit and went down in the target area. Nine to ten chutes were seen from each plane.

Mission 20.
June 22, 1944 - Nucourt, France - 6.30 hrs.
Briefing was held at 12.30. Target was a V-1 site at Nucourt, France. Lieutenant Hank's ship led one of the three groups. There was the usual accurate Flak in the target area. One plane was hit and made a crash landing on the beachhead in France. Two others crash landed in England.

Mission 21.
June 28, 1944 - Denain Prouvy, France - 6 hrs.
Briefing was at 02.30. Target was a tactical one in France. During group take-off, one engine in a B-17 took fire. The crew bailed out, avoiding the explosion when the plane crashed. Target was not visible so the planes bombed a tar-

(continued on page 118)

Right.
On May 7, 1944, Lt. Hanks' crew took part in a mission over Berlin. During the more than nine-hour flight, their plane was badly damaged by Flak and fighters. They limped back to England on three engines, and a stabilizer fin shattered by a stricken German fighter which tried to ram their B-17. The bombardier, Lt. Liakos, was severely wounded. 'Butch II' safely landed but was written off as unrepairable.
(USAAF)

Below.
This photo illustrates clearly the navigational method called the 'Mission Plot Ribbon.' A ribbon was pinned on a map to indicate the main landmarks encountered on the flight. Here, the target is Brest, at the tip of the Brittany peninsula. The outlined areas are major Flak zones: Jersey and Guernsey islands, Brest and its suburbs as well as Lorient further south. On the ribbon, 'IP' means 'Initial Point' and 'T' means 'Target.'
(USAAF)

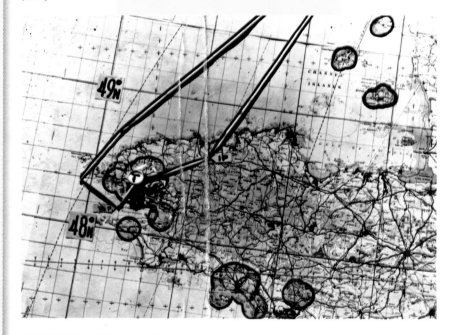

Right.
Damage caused by 20-mm shell from an enemy fighter on a B-17 wing. *(USAAF)*

Right.
Allen Miller's crew in England. The second man standing from the left is Bill Webb, the new bombardier. Near him, Miller and Hanks are wearing ANJ-4 shearling jackets (with patch pockets closed by buttoned flaps). Webb has a B-3 jacket, the rest of the crew have the ubiquitous A-2 leather flight jacket. Their ship is the spanking new 'Toots.'
(USAAF)

Below.
Miller's crew are miming a debriefing by the S-2 (Intelligence) officer after a mission. Two crew members are wearing type A-3 green harnesses. This color was very frequent in comparison with the classical white canvas harnesses. The man in the middle is wearing an A-11 flying helmet, together with a pair of RAF Mk VIII goggles.
(USAAF)

Bottom, left.
This document dated June 5, 1944 issued by the HQ of the 3rd Bombardment Division is a citation representing an additional award of the Air Medal. Miller is allowed to pin a bronze 'oak leaf cluster' (OLC) device on his Air Medal ribbon.

This leaflet with general Eisenhower's message was handed out to all Allied soldiers involved in the Normandy Invasion.

Oak Leaf Cluster to AM   R E S T R I C T E D
GENERAL ORDERS)
                                          Hq 3d Bombardment Division
                                          APO 559
NO. 176   )   E X T R A C T   5 June   1944

Under the provisions of Army Regulations 600-45, 22 September 1943, and pursuant to authority contained in ltr 200.6, Hq. Eighth Air Force, 2 April 1944, subject: "Awards and Decorations," an OAK LEAF CLUSTER is awarded, for wear with the Air Medal previously awarded, to the following-named Officer, organization as indicated, Army Air Forces, United States Army.
Citation: For exceptionally meritorious achievement, while participating in heavy bombardment missions over enemy occupied Continental Europe. The courage, coolness and skill displayed by this Officer upon these occasions reflect great credit upon himself and the Armed Forces of the United States.
*   *   *

ALLEN J. MILLER, O-707087, 2nd Lieutenant, 447th Bombardment Group (H)
*   *
            By command of Major General LE MAY:

OFFICIAL: A. W. KISSNER
                                     Brigadier General, U.S.A.
O. T. DRAEWELL   Chief of Staff
Major, Air Corps
Adjutant General   R E S T R I C T E D

SUPREME HEADQUARTERS
ALLIED EXPEDITIONARY FORCE

Soldiers, Sailors and Airmen of the Allied Expeditionary Force!

You are about to embark upon the Great Crusade, toward which we have striven these many months. The eyes of the world are upon you. The hopes and prayers of liberty-loving people everywhere march with you. In company with our brave Allies and brothers-in-arms on other Fronts, you will bring about the destruction of the German war machine, the elimination of Nazi tyranny over the oppressed peoples of Europe, and security for ourselves in a free world.

Your task will not be an easy one. Your enemy is well trained, well equipped and battle-hardened. He will fight savagely.

But this is the year 1944 ! Much has happened since the Nazi triumphs of 1940-41. The United Nations have inflicted upon the Germans great defeats, in open battle, man-to-man. Our air offensive has seriously reduced their strength in the air and their capacity to wage war on the ground. Our Home Fronts have given us an overwhelming superiority in weapons and munitions of war, and placed at our disposal great reserves of trained fighting men. The tide has turned ! The free men of the world are marching together to Victory !

I have full confidence in your courage, devotion to duty and skill in battle. We will accept nothing less than full Victory !

Good Luck ! And let us all beseech the blessing of Almighty God upon this great and noble undertaking.

Dwight Eisenhower

get of opportunity, the airfield at Denain. Results were rated as good. There were no losses.

Mission 22.
July 11, 1944 - Munich, Germany - 9.15 hrs.
The Charge of Quarters awoke the men scheduled for the mission at 03.30.

By the time they were wide awake and dressed, had some breakfast of fresh eggs, bacon and toast, it was 05.00, daylight and time for the briefing to commence.

The intelligence officer disclosed that the target was the BMW plant at Munich, for the Luftwaffe had to be kept away from the invasion area. Lt. Hank's crew led the entire group and its navigation fell on Miller's shoulders. Take-off started at 07.40. Bombing altitude of 26.000 feet was reached as the formation crossed the Dutch coast.

Approaching the target, Lt. Altman encountered problems, left the formation and made his way to Switzerland, landing safely there. The Flak was heavy. Lt. Jacob's plane was damaged and he headed for Switzerland under fighter escort. The other formations were not bothered by Luftwaffe fighters so the return trip was uneventful.

Mission 23.
July 12, 1944 - Munich, Germany - 9.45 hrs.
Target was Munich again. Briefing was at 07.00. It was hoped that a visual bombing could be made, and more PFF planes were included on this mission. The outbound trip was uneventful. It was with disappointment that the attackers found the target cloud covered.

Flak was thick as usual. The return flight was uneventful as well. The 447th BG returned without losses and started landing at 17.20.

Mission 24.
July 18, 1944 - Cuxhaven, Germany - 6.30 hrs.
Primary target was the oil storage areas near Kiel harbor. As the planes approached the target, they were advised by pathfinders that the area was hidden by clouds, so the decision was made to bomb a coastal target at Cuxhaven in Northern Germany. Bombing was achieved with using PFF equipment. There were no losses.

Mission 25.
July 21, 1944 - Regensburg, Germany - 9.00 hrs
Colonel Harris started the briefing after he had put the men at ease.

When the curtain was removed from the mission map, crews learned that their target was the Messerschmitt aircraft plant at Regensburg in southern Germany. Flak was so thick that "one could walk on it." The targets were visible, results were excellent. All planes returned safely.

Mission 26.
August 11, 1944 - Belfort, France - 9.00 hrs.
Forty crews were ready for briefing. The target was the marshalling yards at Belfort, France. The formations left England at Dover. They made the trip without mishap and released their bombs with excellent results.

Mission 27.
August 26, 1944 - Brest, France - 6.30 hrs
Lieutenant-colonel Wrigglesworth, the new commanding officer, led his first mission flying with lieutenant Hanks' crew. Take off started at 07.30, but the target could not be pinpointed due to the weather, so the planes were recalled and returned to base with their bombload.

Mission 28.
September 8, 1944 - Mainz, Germany - 7.30 hrs.
43 crews took off at 07.40. Hanks led one of the three groups. The target was industrial plants at Mainz. The planes were able to aim visually with good results. Flak was heavy but not accurate. All ships returned safely.

Mission 29.
September 9, 1944 - Serial A, France - 8 hrs.
This mission was code named 'Grassy.' It was in support of the French resistance fighters in Southern France. Planes were loaded with 443 canisters of supplies and leaflets. After they had crossed the front lines, they came down to an altitude of 2.500 feet towards the drop zone 25 miles south of Besançon. Results were rated as good. Landing started at 14.20. No losses.

Mission 30.
September 10, 1944 -Giebelstadt, Germany - 7.30 hrs
Target was an airfield at Giebelstadt near Schweinfurt. One plane carried leaflets in canisters. Planes were able to aim visually with good results.
The return flight was uneventful.

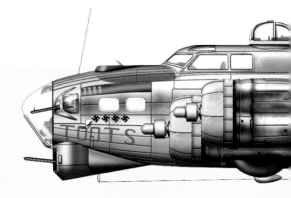

B-17G 'Toots' (serial # 42-107079),
385th BG/708th BS - June 1944.
Lt. Miller flew ten missions
on this plane.
(Computer graphics by Nicolas Gohin)

Below.
During a party at Rattlesden base, Jimmy Doolittle (the 8th AF commanding general) is discussing with colonel Hunter Harris, commanding the 447th BG. Note the 8th AF shoulder patch on the colonel's coat, a typical British embroidered insignia, with 'stubby' wings

Opposite page.
This service coat belonged to a pilot in the 8th Airforce. This captain had ordered if from a London tailor. The 8th Airforce British-made patch is embroidered in yellow (instead of orange) thread on a blue wool backing. The 'Stubby Wings' are typical as well.
(JCP collection)

Left.
After 'Butch II' had been scrapped, Miller's crew was transferred to a B-17 G named 'Toots.' Four aerial victories are painted on the nose of the plane which serial # was 42-107079. Miller's crew flew about ten missions in this plane, particularly the last mission on D-Day.
(RR)

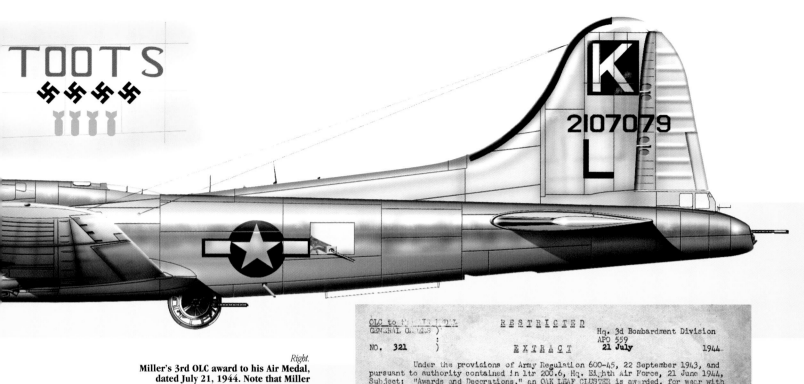

TOOTS

K
2107079
L

Right.
Miller's 3rd OLC award to his Air Medal, dated July 21, 1944. Note that Miller had been promoted to 1st Lieutenant.

Bottom, right.
Allen Miller's flight log sheet for June 1944 totalizing 64.15 flying hours, on 10 missions. Note the two missions on D-Day.

SERVICE COAT OFFICERS
...
Size 37R
BREAST - 37"
WAIST - 32"
S. SIMPSON LTD.
1943
KETTERING FIELD

OLC to
GENERAL ORDERS)   RESTRICTED   Hq. 3d Bombardment Division
)   APO 559
NO. 321   )   EXTRACT   21 July   1944

        Under the provisions of Army Regulation 600-45, 22 September 1943, and
pursuant to authority contained in ltr 200.6, Hq. Eighth Air Force, 21 June 1944,
Subject: "Awards and Decorations," an OAK LEAF CLUSTER is awarded, for wear with
the Air Medal previously awarded, to the following-named Officer, organization
as indicated, Army Air Forces, United States Army.
        Citation: For meritorious achievement while participating in heavy
bombardment missions in the air offensive against the enemy over Continental
Europe. The courage, coolness, and skill displayed by this officer upon these
occasions reflect great credit upon himself and the Armed Forces of the United
States.

 *   *   *   *   *

        ALLEN J. MILLER   O-707087   1st Lieutenant
        708th Bombardment Squadron, 447th Bombardment Group (H)

                      By command of Major General PARTRIDGE:

OFFICIAL:
                                        A. W. KISSNER,
                                        Brigadier General, USA,
                                        Chief of Staff.
F. E. FITZPATRICK,
Captain, Air Corps,
Asst. Adjutant General.

                      RESTRICTED

WAR DEPARTMENT
AAF FORM NO. 5
APPROVED DEC. 7, 1942   INDIVIDUAL FLIGHT RECORD

(1) SERIAL NO. O-707087 (2) NAME MILLER ALLEN J. (3) RANK 2ND LT (4) AGE 1917
(5) PERS. CLASS 18 (6) BRANCH AIR CORPS (7) STATION AAF 126
(8) ORGANIZATION ASSIGNED 8TH 3RD DIV 4TH 447TH 708TH
(10) PRESENT RATING & DATE NAV 12-20-43 (11) ORIGINAL RATING & DATE SAME
MONTH JUNE 1944

DAY	AIRCRAFT TYPE, MODEL & SERIES	NO. LANDINGS	FIRST PILOT DAY P	RATED PERS. NON-PILOT N	INSTRU-MENT N	SPECIAL INFORMATION
2	B-17G	1		4:45		COMBAT #12
3	"	1		5:00		COMBAT #13
5	"	1		1:15		
6	"	1		6:00		COMBAT #14
6	"	1		6:30		COMBAT #15
7	"	1		8:30	2:00	COMBAT #16
12	"	1		6:30		COMBAT #17
10	"			2:00		
14	"	1		6:30		COMBAT #18
16	"			2:00		
18	"	1		8:00		COMBAT #19
18	"			3:00		
22	"	1		6:30		COMBAT #20
27	"			2:30		
25	"			5:00	3:00	
28	"	1		6:00		COMBAT #21

"CERTIFIED CORRECT"

EARL W. NETZEL,
WO (JG), USA,
ASST OPNS OFFICER.

COMBAT TIME THIS MONTH   64:15
PREVIOUS MONTHS   90:45
COMBAT TIME TO DATE   155:00

COLUMN TOTALS   NON   80:00   5:00 NON
                  (42) TOTAL STUDENT PILOT TIME (43) TOTAL FIRST PILOT TIME (44) TOTAL PILOT TIME

(37) THIS MONTH   80:00
(38) PREVIOUS MONTHS THIS F. Y.   301:45
(39) THIS FISCAL YEAR   99:25   381:45
(40) PREVIOUS FISCAL YEARS
(41) TO DATE   99:25   381:45

Above.
The 301st Bomb. Squadron insignia.

Top.
Displaying 27 mission symbols under the cockpit, 'Conquest Cavalier' is pictured in flight in the spring of 1944. This B-24H (serial #41-29196) flew with the 701st BS and was one of the 445th BG's original aircraft. (See color plate on page 122).
(USAAF)

7. 445TH BOMB. GROUP

**701ST BOMB. SQUADRON
SERGEANT JAMES E. PEFLEY
PHOTOGRAPHER**

Constituted as the 445th Bombardment Group (Heavy) on March 20, 1943 with four squadrons (700th, 701st, 702nd and 703rd BS), the group moved to England between October and December 1943 to serve with the Eighth AF.

It was based at Tibenham (USAAF base 124) under the command of colonel Robert H. Terrill and started combat missions on December 13th 1943 by attacking U-boat installations at Kiel. Operated against strategic targets until the

end of the war. Participated in the Allied campaign against the German aircraft industry during the 'Big Week' in February 1944 and was awarded a DUC for raiding an aircraft assembly plant at Gotha on February 24th.

Occasionally, the group flew support missions and helped to prepare for the Invasion by bombing airfields, V-weapon sites, and other targets. On D-Day, the 445th attacked coastal batteries and supported ground forces near Saint-Lô in July 1944.

On July 25th colonel Terrill was replaced by colonel William W. Jones. On September 27th 1944, the group suffered the heaviest losses on a single mission, 24 of its planes were shot down over Kassel.

During the Battle of the Bulge, the unit bombed the German communication network. In March 1945, the unit dropped food, medical supplies and ammunition to troops that landed near Wesel during operation 'Varsity.'

The 445th BG occasionally dropped propaganda leaflets and hauled gasoline to France. The group was awarded the Croix de Guerre with palm by the French government. The unit flew its final combat mission on April 25th 1945 and returned to the USA in May-June, where it was inactivated on September 12, 1945.

From December 13, 1943 to April 25, 1945, the 445th BG lost 108 planes in combat.

Left and above, right.
Sergeant James E. Pefley poses for this classic study, at left in the enlisted men's service uniform and, right, in a B-3 shearling jacket.
(USAAF)

445th Bomb Group

Right.
James Pefley and his fellow students of class 21-43-P 'A' at the USAAF Technical Photography School of Denver (Colo.). Pefley is third from the right, third row.

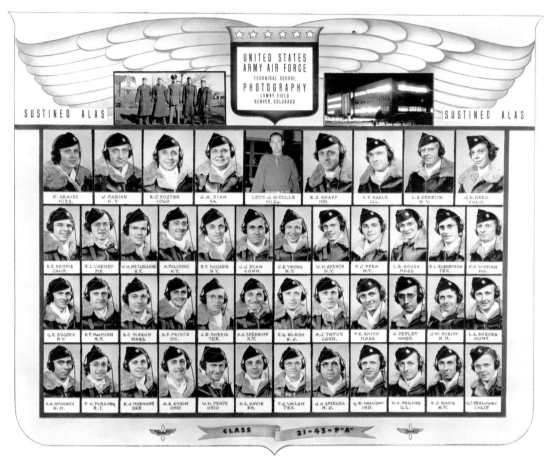

Below.
B-24s of the 445th BG are crossing the coast of occupied Europe. Note on the right wing the identification symbol of the group: a capital F within a disc which was also painted on outer tail surfaces. This marking changed to large black and white horizontal stripes in May 1944.
(USAAF)

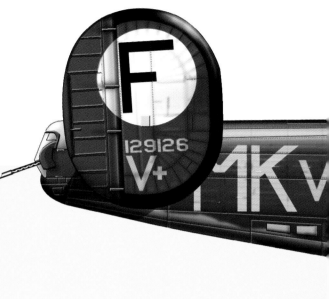

Above, left.
**Several of the 2nd Bomb Division groups employed P-47
Thunderbolt as formation monitor aircraft.
Most of the time, such planes were piloted
by the group commander. The tail bears 445th BG
marking after May 1944: black and white horizontal stripes.
The wing machine guns have been removed to lose weight.**
(USAAF)

Left.
**Photo specialists of the 701st BS on the base,
near one of their photo lab trailers.**
(USAAF)

**This shot illustrates the awesome wingspan
of the B-24 Liberator. Each wing was as long
as the fuselage. The paint finish has worn off
on the walkways for ground crew.**
(USAAF)

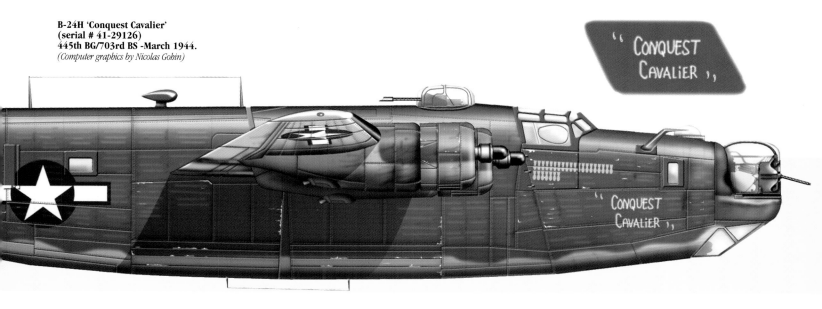

B-24H 'Conquest Cavalier'
(serial # 41-29126)
445th BG/703rd BS -March 1944.
(Computer graphics by Nicolas Gohin)

" CONQUEST CAVALIER ,,

'Georgia Peach' was a P-51C
Mustang escort fighter
fitted with auxiliary tanks,
as seen from
a waist gunner position.
(USAAF)

The 445th BG flight line
at Tibenham.
(USAAF)

These B-24s of the 445th BG are crossing the Channel apparently on the return leg of a mission. Note that one is aluminum-finished, the other camouflaged.
(USAAF)

Most famous aviator at Tibenham was movie star James Stewart, pictured here upon the award of his first Air Medal. For ten months in 1943 and 1944, Tibenham was home to Lt.-col. Stewart.
He flew 20 combat missions as a pilot in B-24 Liberators and was commander of the 703rd Bomb squadron.
Every time Stewart led the group, he never lost an aircraft or a man, quite a record for a unit that consistently suffered heavy losses on many raids. He led the 2nd Bomb. Wing (389th, 445th and 453rd groups) to Berlin on March 22, 1944. Later in 1944 he transferred to the 453rd Bomb Group as operations officer.
He returned to the States as a 'bird' colonel in 1945.
(USAAF)

Below.
A cat is comfortably sleeping on a warrant officer's cap.

Above.
**A 702nd BS B-24
dropping its bombload.**
(USAAF)

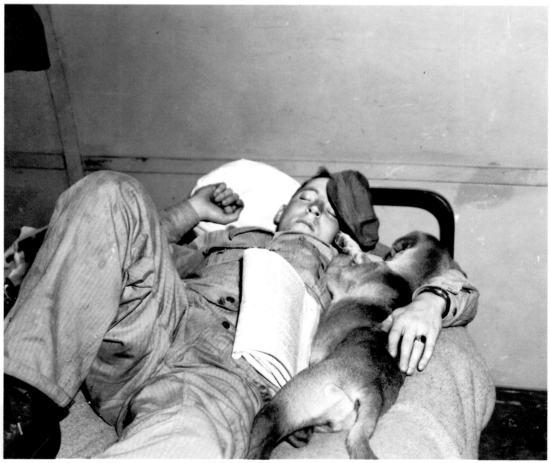

**A technician of the photo lab
in the 445th BG is having
a nap with his pet dog.**

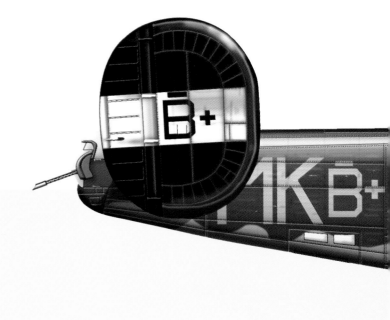

Left.
**Sergeant James Pefley enjoys
a pipe, leaning against
one of the photo lab trailers.**

**Visiting Tibenham airbase,
General James Doolittle
is shown a training device
for gunners.**
(USAAF)

B-24H 'Tahelenbak'
(serial # 42-94921)
445th BG/701st BS - July 1944.
(Computer graphics
by Nicolas Gobin)

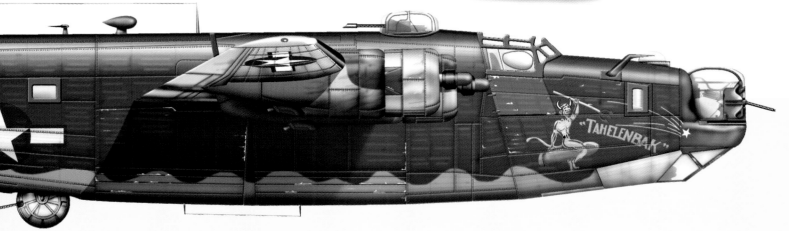

Right.
B-24 'Tahelenbak'
in flight. Note the serial
number painted on the inside
of the tailfin.
This plane survived
the war.
(USAAF)

On Tibenham airbase,
this is another war-weary
Thunderbolt used
as a formation
assembly plane.

NORWICH, ENGLAND
1945

Above.
Sergeant Pefley visits London together with a comrade, a WAC Private first class and a Red Cross Volunteer (center).

Leaflet about the construction of a Memorial Hall dedicated to the men of the 2nd Air Bombardment Division of the 8th AF who died in line of duty. This memorial would have been built in the hall of the town library in Norwich.

Above.
A view of Piccadilly Circus. A specific shelter has been built to protect the statue against bombs.

London cabs near Piccadilly.

Right.
Alighting from a British train car,
this 8th Air Force Major returns to his unit
after a short leave in London. The climate compels him
to keep a raincoat handy, folded on his arm.
He wears the standard officer's 1942-pattern service coat
in olive drab wool elastique material.
The collar sports the arm-of-service insignia of winged
propellers and the U. S monograms.
Rank badges (gilt oak leaves) are pinned
on the shoulder loops, a British-made 8th AF shoulder
patch has been stitched on the sleeve. It has the typical
'Stubby wings' of locally-procured patches.
On the chest are pinned the pilot wings and service ribbons:
Distinguished Flying Cross, Air Medal with OLC devices
and European Campaign medal. On the left, the blue and gilt
Presidential Unit Citation is worn by all personnel of the unit.
Owing to their contrasting hue compared with the shirt
and coat colors, these service trousers are known as 'pinks.'
His service cap is the regulation pattern with stiff crown.
Russet brown low quarters shoes are worn,
these were often purchased from renowned British
shoemakers. His few personal belongings
are packed in a canvas and leather bag.
(Reconstruction, P. Besnard/Le Poilu collection, photo by Militaria Magazine)

129

Private purchase enlisted personnel service coat, tailored in Britain for an Airforce flying NCO. The service cap has been locally-made as well, from British officer service dress wool material. The gunner wings are bullion-embroidered on a blue 'Combat flying duty patch.' Service ribbons are for the following: Air Medal with two oak leaf clusters, Good Conduct Medal and European Campaign Medal with one battle star.
(Overlord Collection)

Left.
James Pefley near the entrance of Madame Tussaud's.

One of the four lions at the foot of Nelson's column on Trafalgar Square, near the National Gallery.

130

8. 389TH BOMB. GROUP

CORPORAL ANNE L. PENNICK
AIR WAC

The 389th Bombardment Group (Heavy) was established on December 19th, 1942 with four squadrons (564, 565, 566 and 567th BS) and was first commanded by colonel David B. Lancaster, then by col. Jack W. Wood as of May 1943. The unit moved to England in June-July 1943, and was based at Hethel (USAAF base 114).

A detachment was immediately sent to Libya, where it began operations in July 1943 over Crete, Sicily, Italy, Austria and Rumania. The group received a DUC for its participation in the famed low-level attack against oil refineries at Ploesti on August 1, 1943. During this operation, 2nd Lt. Lloyd H. Hughes was posthumously awarded the Medal of Honor. Refusing to turn back although gasoline was streaming from his flak-damaged plane, Hughes flew at low altitude over the target area and bombed the objective.

His plane crashed before he could attempt a forced landing after the bomb run. The detachment returned to England in August and the group flew several missions against airfields in France and Holland.

Operating temporarily from Tunisia, September-October 1943, the 389th supported Allied operations at Salerno and hit targets in Corsica, Italy, and Austria. Back in England in October 1943 , until April 1945 the group flew missions against strategic objectives in occupied Europe.

Also participated in the 'Big Week,' February 20-25th, 1944. In March 1944 colonel Arnold was replaced by col. Robert B. Miller. The group also flew support missions on several occasions, bombing gun batteries and airfields during the Normandy invasion, striking enemy positions to aid the breakthrough at Saint-Lô in July.

Col. Ramsay D. Potts took command on August 17, 1944. Hitting depots and communications centers during the Battle of the Bulge, the group also dropped food and ammuni-

Above.
On Hethel airbase, a WAC officer pins a ribbon on a sergeant's blouse. Note the various hairstyles, the typical cut of the garments and hats.

WACs taking the oath at the start of their basic training in the USA. This snapshot was mailed by Anne Pennick to her parents, and she indicated where she stood.

tion, hauled gasoline and other supplies to troops participating in the airborne assault across the Rhine in March 1945. In December 1944, colonel Potts was replaced by colonel John B. Herboth, himself replaced in April by Lt. Col Jack G. Merrell.

The 389th flew its last combat mission late in April 1945. It returned to the USA in May-June 1945 and was inactivated on September 13, 1945. From July 1943 to April 1945, the 389th BG lost 153 B-24s in combat.

C

389th Bomb Group

PRAISES RED CROSS

Corp. Anne L. Pennick of Wacs Now Is Stationed in London

Corp. Anne L. Pennick, daughter of Mr. and Mrs. S. E. Pennick, 409 East Central, who joined the Wac in January, has written that she is

CORP. ANNE L. PENNICK

enjoying her life in London, where she has been stationed since August.

Corporal Pennick stated she and other Wacs in London have been impressed by the job being done by the Red Cross. The girls live in a club provided for them by the Red Cross when they are on furlough from their posts, and "only pay three shillings (about 60 cents) for a room with a lovely soft mattress, white woolen blankets, soft white sheets, lovely drapes on the windows, a dresser in each room, telephone in the hall, clothes closets for each girl and the privilege of sleeping as late as one wants to in the morning."

**Decorative mural painting
in the WAC club
at the 389th base.**

Right.
**A WAC officer rides
a British bike
near the airfield.**

This card vouched
that Sgt. Pennick
was currently assigned
to the 389th BG when
the unit completed
its 300th mission.

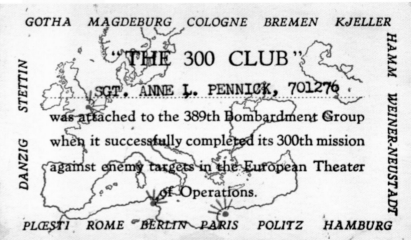

GOTHA   MAGDEBURG   COLOGNE   BREMEN   KJELLER

"THE 300 CLUB"

SGT. ANNE L. PENNICK, 701276

was attached to the 389th Bombardment Group when it successfully completed its 300th mission against enemy targets in the European Theater of Operations.

STETTIN   DANZIG   HAMM   WEINER-NEUSTADT

PLŒSTI   ROME   BERLIN   PARIS   POLITZ   HAMBURG

Above.
**An unusual shot, taken from a B-24 cockpit.
A chaplain blesses a crew before it takes off for a mission.**

Above.
Safely back after a flight, these crew members are gathering
their E-3 survival kits as these have to be returned to the supply room.
Three are wearing B-11 parkas and A-10 flying trousers.
Note their modified A-6 flying boots and the plugs
of the type F-3 electrically-heated suits.

Below.
These crew members in heavy flying suits or electrically heated
underwear are waiting for the last meteorological update before boarding.
Note the M-3 Flak helmet at the feet of the man far left and the F-2 black felt shoes
of the nearest man. The latter shows a less than flattering figure,
owing to the many layers of warm clothing under his flying suit.

384th Bomb Group

The 384th Bomb. Group insignia.

It assisted the Allied assault across the Rhine in March 1945 (operation 'Varsity' by cutting off enemy supplies. The 384th remained in Europe after V-E Day. Its planes ferried GIs to Casablanca for shipment to the USA, carried Greek soldiers to their homeland, and moved troops to Germany.

The group was inactivated in France on February 28th 1946. From June 1943 to April 1945, on 314 missions, the 384th BG lost 159 planes in action.

Bombardier wings.

Navigator wings. This was Stern's official function on most of his combat flights.

9. 384TH BOMB. GROUP

545TH BOMB. SQUADRON
1ST LT. HAROLD STERN

GUNNER - BOMBARDIER - NAVIGATOR
35 MISSIONS

Constituted as the 384th Bombardment Group on November 25th 1942 with four squadrons (544th, 545th, 546th and 547th BS), the unit moved to England in May-June 1943, and was assigned to the Eighth AF. From its base at Grafton Underwood (USAAF base #106), the group was part of the strategic bombardment organization, and struck airfields and industries in France and Germany.

The 384th received a first DUC for a damaging raid on aircraft factories in central Germany on January 11th 1944. As many other heavy bombardment groups of the 8th AF, the 384th took part in the 'Big Week' (February 20th -25th 1944). It received another DUC for its April 24, 1944 mission when it led the 41st Wing through overwhelming opposition to attack an aircraft factory and airfield at Oberpfaffenhofen.

The unit suffered heavy losses of men and planes. Until the end of the war, the 384th bombed different types of strategic targets: ports, communication centers, oil facilities, cities, marshalling yards… as well as tactical support missions. In June 1944, the group attacked installations along the coast of Normandy prior to and during the Invasion. Then it bombed airfields and communications beyond the beachhead and supported ground troops during operation 'Cobra.'

In September 1944, the 384th hit tank and gun concentrations around Eindhoven to support airborne troops in operation 'Market Garden' in Holland. During the Battle of the Bulge (Dec. 1944-Jan. 1945), the unit struck enemy communications and fortifications.

Above.
Harold Stern in the Air Cadet officer-like uniform. Note the gunner wings and the Marksman badge on his chest. Stern had originally enlisted as a private in the Air Corps in Dec. 1942.

Below.
Unofficial gunner diploma awarded to Harold Stern on December 11th 1943 at Kingman airbase in Arizona.

Stateside training: Stern is standing second from left, wearing a summer flying suit. Two gunners are showing off ammo belts on their shoulders.

Various insignia and items which belonged to Harold Stern:
- A leather name tag for the flying jacket,
- Two Air Medals (one privately engraved on the back),
- Army Marksman badge with 'pistol' bar,
- British-made ribbon bar with oak leaf clusters on the Air Medal,

– Shirt-size Gunner wings. Stern enlisted as a private and first trained as a gunner in the Airforce before entering the Air Cadet scheme.
– Regulation size Bombardier wings (non-hallmarked),
– Officer Dog tag,
– Bracelet fashioned out of British Three Pence coins.

"*New AAF Bombardier is 2nd Lieutenant Harold M. Stern, shown above with his wife (right) and her sister and mother, all of Yonkers, following his graduation from the bombardier school at the Carlsbad, N.M., Army Air Field. A triple threat man, he had gunnery training at another AAF Training Command school before receiving bombardier-navigation training at Carlsbad.*"

Top, right.

Observer Bombardier diploma made out for Harold Stern on June 10th 1944 at Carlsbad Air Field. Stern was still an Air Cadet and retained his enlisted man's Army serial number.

Harold Stern's officer calling card and the invitation and program of the graduation ceremony at Carlsbad Bombardier School.

On Grafton Underwood airbase, armorers are checking a bombload before it is carried to the planes.
(USAAF)

A high altitude flight of 384th BG B-17s.
(USAAF)

Stern's crew is posing under the nose of their B-17G,
which has already flown many missions as shown by the bombs
painted on the nose. Stern is at far right. Far left,
two officers are wearing B-15 jackets.

HAROLD STERN'S MISSIONS

A SUMMARY OF THIS AIRMAN'S MISSIONS BETWEEN 5 NOV. 1944 AND 16 APRIL 1945, AS EXTRACTED FROM HIS HANDWRITTEN DIARY

Mission 1.
Nov 5th, 1944 -Frankfurt, Germany
Railroad marshalling yards.
Plenty of Flak. Holes in nose and cockpit, about 15 in all. Kind of rough for first mission. Home safe.

Mission 2.
Nov 6th, 1944 - Bottrop, Germany
Five miles from Essen.
Synthetic oil plant. Not too rough. Lots of 51's and 47's for escort. Home safe.

Mission 3.
Nov 8th, 1944 - Merseburg, Germany
60 miles from Berlin. One of the largest synthetic oil plants in Germany. Lost one engine 10 minutes from Initial Point. Salvoed bombs and turned back alone.
Second engine out on way back. Had to fly 250 miles across Germany alone. Two Me 109's trailed us for thirty minutes until we got to Netherlands.
We ducked through clouds to avoid them. Had Flak in and out getting 4 holes in right wing, one in number 2 engine. Was sure a rough mission.
Home safe Thank God. Landed at Great Ashfield, returned to Grafton Underwood next day.

Mission 4.
Nov 11th, 1944 - Gelsenkirchen, Germany
Synthetic oil plant. Had lots of 51's and plenty of Flak around target. Not too bad as we had 10/10 cloud cover and Flak was inaccurate. Flew hot camera ship. Home safe and still thank God and Joy's prayers.

Mission 5.
Nov 16th, 1944 - Eschweiler, Germany
Tactical support of ground troops. We bombed between Metz and Essen to pave way for the start of the big push into Germany. Had some Flak and rockets. Our group was commended by Gen. Doolittle for a good job.

Mission 6.
Nov 20th, 1944 - Munster, Germany
Bombed rail yards through complete cover and undercast. Lots of P-51 protection. Sweated out an uneventful mission. Home safe as usual. Do a lot of Joy's prayers asking God to watch over us.

NAME: Stern, Harold M.   AWARDS

Awarded AM for meritorious achievement, GO # 558 Hq 1st BD. 11-24-44
Awarded OLC for meritorious achievement, GO # 93 Hq 1st AD. 2-1-45
Awarded OLC for meritorious achievement, GO # 222 Hq 1st AD. 3-14-45
Awarded OLC for meritorious achievement, GO # 249 Hq 1st AD. 3-24-45
Awarded OLC for meritorious achievement, GO # 286 Hq 1st AD. 4-5-45
Awarded OLC for meritorious achievement, GO # 328 Hq 1st AD. 4-18-45

Has completed the following sorties over enemy occupied Europe as confirmed by CO 384th Bomb Group (H)

11-5-44	Frankfurt, Germany	3-18-45	Berlin, Germany
11-6-44	Bottrop, Germany	3-19-45	Pluen, Germany
11-8-44	Merseburg, Germany	3-20-45	Hamburg, Germany
11-11-44	Gelsenkirchen, Germany	3-23-45	Gladbeck, Germany
11-16-44	Eschweiler, Germany	3-24-45	Vchta, Germany
11-20-44	Munster, Germany	3-26-45	Meinden, Germany
12-24-44	Kifch Gons, Germany	3-28-45	Berlin, Germany
12-28-44	Bruhl, Germany	3-31-45	Halle, Germany
1-1-45	Derben, Germany	4-3-45	Kiel, Germany
1-7-45	Blankheim, Germany	4-4-45	Fassberg, Germany
1-20-45	Mannheim, Germany	4-6-45	Leipzig, Germany
1-29-45	Siegen, Germany	4-7-45	Hitzacker, Germany
3-2-45	Rositz, Germany	4-9-45	Furstenfelderuck, Germany
3-3-45	Hanover, Germany	4-16-45	Regensburg, Germany
3-7-45	Giessen, Germany		
3-8-45	Essen, Germany		
3-9-45	Kassel, Germany		
3-11-45	Bremen, Germany		
3-12-45	Betzdorf, Germany		
3-14-45	Minden, Germany		
3-17-45	Erfurt, Germany		

B-17Gs of the 545th Bomb squadron over Germany. The group marking on the fin is a white triangle and black 'P' outlined in black for better visibility over the aluminum finish. The squadron code is 'JD.'
(USAAF)

Above.
Over target, 1,000 pound bombs are dropped in a bunch.
(USAAF)

B-15 flying jacket
and close up
of the
manufacturer's tag.

JACKET, INTERMEDIATE, FLYING
TYPE B-15
SPECIFICATION NO.2302 FS
STOCK NO. 813-47963
ORDER NO. 44-6955
FITZWELL SPORTSWEAR,INC
ORIGINAL TYPE
U.S. ARMY AIR FORCES

POLAROID
FLYING GOGGLE,
A.A.F. TYPE B-8
T.M. REG. U.S. PAT. OFF.

RADIO OPERATOR - MARCH 1945

12 March 1945. Crewmen of the 384th
Bomb. Group are back from a raid on the
Betzdorf marshalling yards. Near his
ship, this radio operator computes the
mission's flight time while waiting for
the truck that will take him and the crew
to the barracks and the Intelligence
officer debriefing.

Our man's flying gear is as follows:
– Royal Air Force 1944-pattern flying
helmet fitted with American ANB-H1
earphones
– A-14 oxygen mask
with ANB-MC-1 mike
– B-8 goggles ;
– B-15 flying jacket ;
– B-4 life preserver ;
– AN-6550 flying suit ;
– Modified A-6 sheepskin-lined boots ;
– F-3 heated gloves ;
– F-3 electrically-heated suit,
worn under the regular
flying suit. Cable and plug
are visible at left ;
– AN-6513-1A parachute harness.
The NCO holds an E3-A escape
and survival kit, that had
to be turned in at
the supply room.
(Reconstruction, photo Militaria Magazine)

B-8 flying goggles.
(M. Bianchi photo and collection)

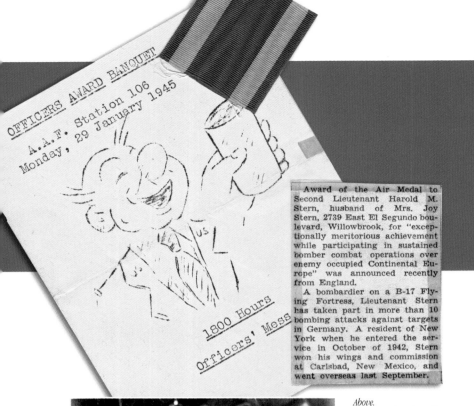

OFFICERS AWARD BANQUET
A.A.F. Station 106
Monday, 29 January 1945

1800 Hours
Officers' Mess

Award of the Air Medal to
Second Lieutenant Harold M. Stern, husband of Mrs. Joy Stern, 2739 East El Segundo boulevard, Willowbrook, for "exceptionally meritorious achievement while participating in sustained bomber combat operations over enemy occupied Continental Europe" was announced recently from England.
A bombardier on a B-17 Flying Fortress, Lieutenant Stern has taken part in more than 10 bombing attacks against targets in Germany. A resident of New York when he entered the service in October of 1942, Stern won his wings and commission at Carlsbad, New Mexico, and went overseas last September.

Above.
Program for the officers' award banquet dated January 29th 1945. The press cutting reports Harold Stern's Air Medal award after completing 10 combat missions. The swatch of Air Medal ribbon was added in the medal box to be mounted on a bar.

Left.
Howard Stern pictured at his navigation table. The cold and altitude have altered this shot's quality.

Operating during daylight bombing missions with USAAF planes as of February-March 1945, RAF Lancasters are photographed in action.
(USAAF)

Mission 7.
Dec 24th, 1944 - Kirchgons, Germany
Bombed a Luftwaffe field near Frankfurt and really demolished it. Lots of rockets and Flak around us. Saw a few jet planes. We had lot of P-51s around us. Was a good mission and my first as a navigator. Did OK. Home safe. Thank God.

Mission 8. Dec 28th, 1944 - Brühl, Germany
Bombed rail yards near Cologne. 10/10 clouds and not much Flak. Lot of P-51's. Pretty good mission. Home safe. Thank God.

Mission 9.
January 1, 1945 - Derben, Germany
What a New Year! Went to bomb an oil dump near Hamburg but due to a screw up took a Cook's tour through the heart of Germany and finally bombing Kassel thru intense Flak.
We had God with us because in 6 hours over Germany no fighters appeared, and if they had we would have had it as our P-51's were not. We passed near Hamburg, Hanover, Berlin, Coblenz etc…
These are the roughest spots over there. We had lot of Flak at the target, but thank God back home OK with just a few holes in our ship.

Mission 10.
January 7, 1945 - Blankenheim, Germany
Support of ground troops. Bombed nazi ground concentrations. 10/10 clouds. Nice mission - No Flak. Home Safe.

Mission 11.
January 20, 1945 - Mannheim, Germany
Railroad bridge. Mission went well. Some Flak. Weather was rough. Clouds to 30,000 feet. Temperature: - 60° c. Came back to base but was diverted.
Ceiling on ground. Snow ice in clouds. Was treated very nice. Back home next day.

Mission 12.
January 29, 1945 - Siegen, Germany
Railroad yards. A long haul but a good one. Plenty of our own fighter support and lot of clouds to hide us from the Flak.
Bombed troops trains and yards. Going to help Russia this way more often they tell us.

Mission 13.
March 2, 1945 - Rositz, Germany
Synthetic oil plant. Ten hours trip. Lot of Flak over target. Five holes in plane.
Ran out of gas and landed in Merville in France for more. Arrived at home base safe two hours late.

Mission 14.
March 3, 1945 - Hannover, Germany
Had a long trip over North sea. Hit target. Lot of intense and accurate Flak.
Flew back and more Flak at Holland coast. Jet plane. Got home safe. Thank God.

Mission 15.
March 7, 1945 - Geissen, Germany
Geissen railroad yards - Bombed PFF. Weather bad. Two runs on target. Home Safe. Thank God

Mission 16.
March 8, 1945 - Essen, Germany
Bombed railroad yards and town. Good mission, little Flak. All went well. Home safe.

Mission 17.
March 9, 1945 - Kassel, Germany
Bombed tank factory. Visual. Saw target from Initial Point. Smoke screen over it but not good. Plenty of Anti-aircraft guns shooting at us.
Could see hundreds of gun flashes on ground. Flew through heavy Flak barrage over town. Got a few holes in plane. Rest of trip was OK. Home safe.

Mission 18.
March 11, 1945 - Bremen, Germany
Bombed sub pens. 10/10 clouds. Lot of Flak. Pretty good mission. Back OK. Thank God.

Mission 19.
March 12, 1945 - Betzdorf, Germany
Bombed railroad yards. Good mission.
No Flak for a change.
All went well. Home safe.

Mission 20.

**Harold Stern's 'chenille'
British-made
545th Bomb
Squadron patch.**

EIGHTH
AIR FORCE

.R. NAVIGATION   CERTIFICATE

**Certificate given to 8th AF qualified dead reckoning
navigators. This document proves that crew training
was not always completed in the USA.**

HEADQUARTERS EIGHTH AIR FORCE
AAF STATION 101
APO 634

C E R T I F I C A T E

DATE 15ᵀᴴ JANUARY 1945

This is to certify that ₁ₙ₀ G. HAROLD M. STERN, O-780275 Bombardier,
satisfactorily completed a course of instruction in accordance with Eighth
e Memorandum 50-7, is qualified to act as NAVIGATOR on flights involving
of dead reckoning navigation, pilotage, and the use of radio aids.

The course of instruction has included the following:

a. **Ground Instruction**

(1)	Map reading	2 hours
(2)	Dead reckoning navigation; plotting and measuring courses	4 hours
(3)	Log-book procedure; the flight plan	2 hours
(4)	Radio Aids to Navigation	4 hours
(5)	Code (A standard of six words per minute)	
(6)	Use of the radio compass and plotting fixes	3 hours
(7)	Identification and emergency procedures	1 hour
(8)	Compasses and Magnetism	2 hours
(9)	Theory of Gee and its operation	5 hours

b. **Flying Training.** A minimum of 15 hours flying as navigator on
following has been accomplished:

(1) One radio fix taken and plotted every 30 minutes.
(2) Drift readings taken every 10 minutes and winds determined
    on all legs of flight.
(3) Complete log-book kept with all navigational data entered.
(4) Demonstrated ability to pin-point by map-reading.
(5) Demonstrated ability to take and plot fixes, using Gee.

c. **Examination.** Satisfactory grade (80 per cent) on Sections 1, 2,
3 and 5 of Examination given in Section 2, Group Navigator's Handbook, issued by
this Headquarters.

By command of Lieutenant General DOOLITTLE:

E. W. MASCHMEYER
Colonel, A.C.
Executive, A-3

Commanding Officer
384TH Bombardment Group.

Group Navigator.
CAPT. A.C.

Eighth Air Force Navigator.
Major   A.C.

Right.
**No less than 23 hours of detailed courses
and 15 hours of training in flight were necessary
for Harold Stern to be qualified as a DR Navigator.
The certificate was issued under the authority
of general Doolittle, and signed by the 384th BG CO,
the 8AF and group navigators as well
as by the executive 'operations' officer.**

March 14, 1945 - Minden, Germany
Bombed railroad bridge. Some Flak. Crossed Rhine. Saw Coblenz near bridgehead. Plenty of our fighters around. Home safe.

Mission 21.
March 17, 1945 - Erfurt - Leipzig, Germany
A long mission but a fairly easy one. Lot of clouds and crummy weather. Some Flak. Home safe and tired.

Mission 22.
March 18, 1945 - Berlin, Germany
Bombed railroad yards in center of town. Lot of accurate Flak and fighters in area, but thank goodness they didn't get us. Plenty of P-51s for escort. Pretty long haul but home safe. Thank God.

Mission 23.
March 19, 1945 - Pluen, Germany
A long haul and a rough one. Flew through heavy clouds. Lost formation for a while over target.
Jet planes around us, but finally bombed town and got home safe.
Thank God and my wife's prayers.

Mission 24. March 20, 1945 - Hamburg, Germany
Bombed docks and sub pens.
Lot of Flak and attacks by jet planes. Visual and saw lot of stuff on ground.
Home safe. Thank God.

Mission 25. March 23, 1945 - Gladbeck, Germany
In the Ruhr. Hit railroad yards. Visual. Lot of Flak. Lost 2 ships in squadron. Got home safe.

Mission 26. March 24, 1945 - Vechta, Germany
We hit airfield and ruined it. No Flak except on Holland coast. Nice mission.
Home safe. Thank God

Mission 27.
May 26, 1945 - Meiningen, Germany
Made 4 runs on target starting at Leipzig.
Bad weather, no Flak.
Home safe from long mission.

Mission 28.
March 28, 1945 - Berlin, Germany
Long mission, bad weather. Bombed tank factory.
Moderate Flak.
Home safe on 3 engines.

Mission 29.
March 31, 1945 - Halle, Germany
Bombed town. Little Flak. Punk weather.
Home safe, thank God.

Mission 30.
April 3, 1945 - Kiel, Germany
Bombed docks and sub pens. Plenty of Flak. Long trip over North sea. Home safe.

Mission 31.
April 4, 1945 - Fassberg, Germany
Bombed airfield full of Ju-88s and Me-110s. Really plastered it. Long mission.
Some Flak.
Home safe.

Mission 32.
April 6, 1945 - Leipzig, Germany
Bombed railroad yards.
Good mission. Long one.
Home safe. Thank God.

Mission 33.
April 7, 1945 - Hitzacker, Germany
Bombed oil storage dumps.
Visual. Good mission. No Flak.

Mission 34.
April 9, 1945 - Furstenfelderuck, Germany
Bombed rail yards.
Some Flak.
Long mission. Home safe, thank God.

Mission 35.
April 16, 1945 - Regensburg, Germany
Bombed rail yards. A little Flak, long ride. My last mission and a good one.
Home safe. Thank God and Joy's prayers.

A formation of the 384th BG is pictured over a thick cloud cover. The sunlight reflection on clouds and plane fuselages gives a particular light to this shot. *(USAAF)*

Harold Stern's individual flight record sheet for March 1945. March proved particularly busy for the 8th Air Force. Stern flew 17 missions during this month (half of his complete tour). Note that the second flight on March 2nd and those on the 6th, 25th and 27th were not counted as combat missions. They probably were training flights or canceled missions.

*"One of the 384th BG mascots
perches on the shoulders
of one of her favorites,
Lt. Harold Stern,
a Fortress navigator,
on his return."*
(Planet News Ltd)

Bottom right.
**Bombardment of a fuel dump
in Germany.**
(USAAF)

**Accurate bombardment
of railways.**
(USAAF)

29 February 1944, just after the 'Big Week' (see page 29).
This B-17F nicknamed 'Censored' (serial# 42-29897)
was assigned to the 524th BS and bore the ID code WA-A.
The crew members are not identified.
This ship survived the war and returned to the USA.
(USAAF)

10. 379TH BOMB. GROUP

379th Bomb Group

ANONYMOUS PHOTO ALBUM

Above.

Established on October 28, 1942, the 379th Bomb. Group boasted 4 squadrons (524, 525, 526 & 527th BS). It moved to England flying the North Atlantic route in April 1943, under the command of Colonel Maurice A. Preston. Operations began May 19, 1943 and the group was committed to the strategic bombing scheme over occupied Europe.

The 379th received a Distinctive Unit Citation for its operations from May to July 1943, and a second one for flying unescorted into Central Germany to attack large aeronautical concerns on January 11, 1944.

The 379th BG bombed positions just ahead of the assault forces on June 6, 1944 and struck enemy units in July to assist ground troops in the Saint-Lô breakthrough.

Attacked German communications and build-ups during the Battle of the Bulge from December 1944 to January 1945. Bombed bridges and viaducts in France and Germany to aid the Rhine crossing.

After V-E day, the 379th BG moved to French Morocco where it was inactivated in June 1945. From May 1943 to April 1945, the 379th BG lost 141 planes in action.

The 379th Bomb Group insignia.

This picture of Lt. Stewart's crew was taken on August 31, 1943 at Kimbolton airbase in England. They belonged to the 524th Bomb Squadron and flew most of their 25 missions on a B-17 named 'Al-Jo-Son'(serial # 42-5830, coded WA-T). This plane was later renamed 'Hag of Hardewyk.' The B-17 behind them was probably not their ship as its individual letter is 'R.' These were the crew's names and battle stations:
2nd Lt. Carson Stewart Jr. (pilot),
2nd Lt. Richard Ralston (co-pilot),
2nd Lt. Irving Hudson (navigator),
2nd Lt. George E. Beeman (bombardier),
T/Sgt. Robert H. Terrell (radio operator/gunner),
T/Sgt. Harry D. Brunette (top turret gunner),
S/Sgt. Ray W. Dawson (ball turret gunner),
T/Sgt. Thomas H. Jones Jr. (starboard waist gunner),
S/Sgt. Roger C. Riteour (port waist gunner),
S/Sgt. Clyde F. Needing (tail gunner).
(USAAF)

BOMBARDIER - AUGUST 1943

August 9, 1943 on Kimbolton airbase, this bombardier
of the 379th Bomb. group is about to take his station within the bomber's nose.
Target for that day was the enemy airfield at Vitry-en-Artois, France.

The officer wears a thick shearling flight suit of B-3 jacket, A-3 trousers, A-6 boots
and A-9 gloves. The issue wool knit scarf and rayon glove liners top off his flying
clothing and ensure protection against the cold.
The F-1 heated suit is also worn underneath.
The jacket has large horsehide patches to prevent wear at critical spots,
a wide patch pockets is located on the right front.
The A-3 sheepskin-lined trousers feature large patch pockets on the knees.
The full-length zippers on the legs are meant to put them on and off quickly,
especially in case of landing in water.
The chest-pack parachute harness is the standard AN-6513-1A type.
The chest pack is stowed inside the bomber's nose,
within grasp in case of emergency.

The A-6 lined boots have the 1944 modification: and added strap on the shaft top.
The instep strap is missing here, it had probably not been deemed necessary
by the supply room riggers.

(Reconstruction, photo Militaria Magazine)

Above.

**Flying headgear: B-6 flying helmet
with flat hooks for the compatible
oxygen masks (A8-B or A-9).**
The leather strap is lined with
sheepskin under the chin.
The green soft rubber A8-B
was a 'continuous flow' oxygen mask.
This obsolete and fragile equipment
was replaced during 1943
by better masks.
Flying goggles are the Skyway
commercial pattern, purchased
'off the shelf' by the Airforce.
They were liked on account
of their comfort and synthetic
non-shatter eyepieces.
Radio accessories are the T-30V
throat mike and ANB-H1 earphones
on a leather covered metal
headband and gray
foam rubber earcups.
(Reconstruction, photo by Militaria Magazine)

On the 379th BG airbase
in England, two Soviet military
attachés escorted
by an Airforce officer examine
a B-17's twin tail MGs.
(USAAF)

An armorer
is boresighting
the twin 50 cal. machine
guns of a B-17 G's
distinctive chin turret.
(USAAF)

Lieutenant Joseph Theiss' crew was pictured
on July 16, 1943 in front of B-17 F
'Stump Jumper' (serial# 42-30237 - code WA-V)
after a mission on Hannover.
(USAAF)

July 16, 1943:
the flight engineer/gunner
of the crew #80 is sitting
on the top turret which
he manned during
fighter attacks.
(USAAF)

Above and below.
Most of the time,
aircraft maintenance
was carried out outdoors,
whatever the weather
and temperature.
Only major repairs were
made in lighted hangars
in which ground crews
worked nonstop.
(USAAF)

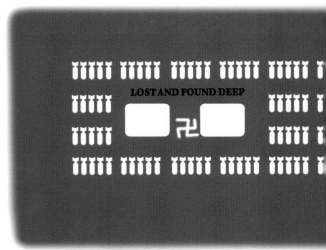

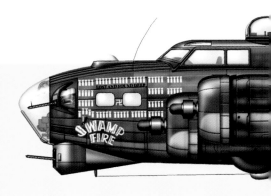

Above.
Clutching a bottle in celebration, a mechanic is painting the white bomb symbolizing the 100th mission of 'Swamp fire.'
(USAAF)

B-17G 'Swamp Fire'
(serial # 42-32024).
379th BG/524th BS -
November 1944.
This bomber was the first
of the 8th AF to reach
100 missions.
*(Computer graphics
by Nicolas Gohin)*

Previous page, bottom.
A historical record for the 8th AF: 'Swamp Fire' of the 524th BS was the first 8th AF plane
to complete 100 missions without ever having to abort due to mechanical mishaps.
The hundredth was a mission to Gelsenkirchen, Germany, on January 11, 1944. These were
the B-17's crew and stations: 1st Lt. Bruce Mills Jr. (pilot), 2nd Lt. Carl Shedlock (co-pilot),
2nd Lt. John McCray (navigator), 2nd Lt. James Whitney (bombardier), T/Sgt. Joseph Cooper
(radio operator/gunner), T/Sgt. Delmer Menger (flight engineer/top turret gunner),
S/Sgt. James Boston (ball turret gunner), S/Sgt. Lucas Conner (waist gunner),
S/Sgt. William Beddard Jr. (tail gunner).
(USAAF)

Right.
The crew members of 'Swamp Fire' wore
their ship's name painted on the back of their flight jackets.
(USAAF)

B-17 F 'Dangerous Dan' (serial# 42-29891, code WA-N) with Lt. Kenneth Davis
at the controls, crash-landed in Ubbeston, Suffolk, after a mission to Osnabrück,
Netherlands, on December 22, 1943.

Left and right.
November 26, 1943: this pilot is celebrating his final mission before rotating back to the USA. He seems happy to be alive, for this mission was eventful, as the battle damage on a wing proves. The officer is wearing an electrically-heated F-1 suit ('Blue Bunny Suit') by itself, while the suit was normally worn under heavier clothing. This was currently observed in several 8th AF bomb groups.
(USAAF)

A printed escape map of Northern Europe (sector C/D) serves as a backdrop for this display:
- Waterproofed canvas pouch for the escape kit. The initials C/D or E/F indicate which maps are inside. Other contents were: a miniature compass, a saw blade and banknotes from several Occupied European nations
- 100 Francs bills
- Escape map of sector E/F
- RAF whistle (hallmarked 'Air Ministry')
- English/French phrase book
- English/German phrase book
- Manual for POWs
- ESM/1 signal mirror
- E-17 escape kit with compass and assorted medical and energy food items
- Aerial chart board.

Right.
The AN-42N2004 chest parachute pack.

150

B-17 PILOT, NOVEMBER 1943

November 5, 1943. B-17 crews of the 379th BG are getting ready for a raid on Gelsenkirchen in Germany. The target are marshalling yards and an oil plant.

The plane captain wears the F-1 heated suit ('Blue Bunny Suit') by itself with no other clothing over it. He is holding a map board with a chart indicating heavy Flak areas.
The rest of his gear is as follows:
- Officer's garrison cap
  with bullion lieutenant's bar
- B-3 inflatable life jacket
- Early type AN-42N2004 chest parachute pack
- Pattern 40 RAF lined boots and bail-out
  oxygen bottle.
- A-9 thick flying gloves
- Regulation wool scarf.
(Reconstruction, photo by Militaria Magazine)

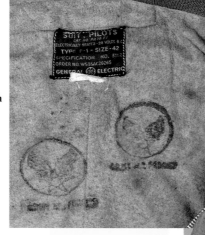

Details of the F-1
electrically-heated
suit's markings
and manufacturer's tag.

THE F-1 ELECTRICALLY-HEATED SUIT

In 1942-43, this remained the only protection against the extreme cold on high altitude flights in non-pressurized bombers. It superseded the older E-1 suit in gray material. Powered by a 24-volt supply, the blue F-1 suit was manufactured in large numbers by the General Electric Corp. and commonly worn within 8th AF bomb groups.

It was fitted with zippers at the cuff and ankle so it could be easily slipped on and dried after the flight. Rubber-encased plugs at the wrist and lower leg were for wiring-in heated D-1 gloves and E-1 booties. For an unknown reason, the latter two were not provided in sufficient numbers and local solutions were prevalent. Electrical gloves and boots (also in 24-volt) were thus obtained from the RAF and modified with American type plugs and sockets.

While it allowed the Airforce to catch up with the other belligerents' flight equipment, the F-1 suit suffered several drawbacks. The wire resistance proved too thin, it often became severed and caused either stinging through the wool material or short circuits.

B-3 inflatable
life jacket.

The 'Aerial Circus' was a Royal Air Force demonstration unit which visited Allied bases to display captured German warbirds in flight. A Ju. 88 and an Me. 110 are examined by 379th BG personnel on January 6, 1944.
(USAAF)

May 24, 1944 was a mission to Berlin for the 524th BS. Target was an aircraft component plant. Mechanics are pictured in front of a plane whose tail was damaged by enemy fighters as it was approaching the target. Once again, this did not prevent the B-17 from flying safely back to base.
(USAAF)

Below, right.
The 524th Bomb Squadron had a big party on October 12, 1943 and enlisted men were crowding around the beer barrels.
(USAAF)

Flying Fortress 'Judy B' (serial # 42-29866, coded WA-L), was named after the baby daughter of Lt. Willis Carlisle, who died at the controls of this ship over Hamburg in July 1943. This bomber was later shot down during a mission over Le Bourget airfield outside Paris on August 16, 1943, with Lt. Biggler (Carlisle's best friend) at the wheel. Of the 10 crew members, 5 were killed, 4 escaped and the last was taken prisoner.
(USAAF)

Above.
A captured Fw. 190, the scourge of bombers
over the Reich, is under close scrutiny
by aircrews and ground personnel.
(USAAF)

July 31, 1943. To celebrate the 'Lawn Fete,'
the 379th BG met the locals who lived around the base.
Note the publican's license
to sell beer.
(USAAF)

Captain Glenn Miller and his AAF band
performed on two matinee concerts in a hangar
at Station 117 (Kimbolton) on August 2, 1944.
(USAAF)

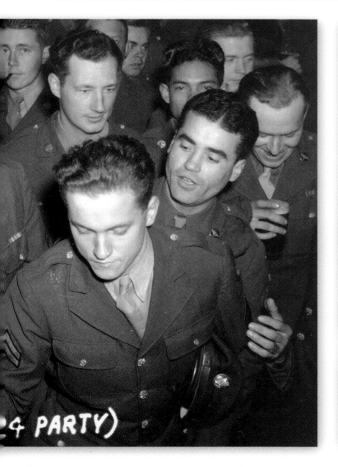

GD-7d-1-467)(31-10-44)(CREW 76 - 145)

11. 467TH BOMB. GROUP

790TH BOMB. SQUADRON
S/SGT. LEE MALUS
GUNNER
30 MISSIONS

The 467th Bombardment Group with its four squadrons (788th, 789th, 790th and 791st Bomb. Squadrons) was constituted on May 29th 1943. Colonel Glantzberg commanded of the unit until October 24th 1943 when he was assigned as Group Commander of the 461st BG. Lt. Colonel Shower took his place and was the only group commander to lead the same unit from the beginning of its operations until V-E Day. In February and March 1944, planes of the Group flew to Morrison Field, Florida to begin the oversea flight via the Southern Ferry Route. Rackheath in England became their base (station #145), five miles northeast of Norwich, Norfolk.

The 467th began its operations on April 10th 1944 with an attack on a Luftwaffe airfield at Bourges in France. The unit took part in the strategic bombing offensive, striking the harbor at Kiel, chemical plants at Bonn, textile factories at Stuttgart, power plants at Hamm, steel works at Osnabrück, aircraft factories at Brunswick, and many other objectives. In addition to these operations, the 467th BG was committed occasionally to support missions. It bombed coastal strongpoints and bridges near Cherbourg on D-Day, enemy troop and supply concentrations near Montreuil (France) on July 25th 1944.

Its B-24s hauled gasoline in September to support the armored divisions' sweep across France. During the Battle of the Bulge, the group attacked German communications and fortifications. Then, the group hit enemy transportation

Sterling silver gunner wings.

The 467th Bomb. Group Insignia.

to assist the Allied assault across the Rhine in March 1945. The 467th flew its last combat mission on April 25th 1945 and returned to the USA in June-July to be inactivated only on August 4th 1946. The 467th boasted the best standards of bombing accuracy in the 8th Air Force. Between April 1944 and April 1945, the 467th BG lost a total of 48 B-24s.

One of the 467th machines, its crew and ground team became celebrities: the 'Witchcraft.' This B-24H of the 790th BS (serial #42-52534) flew a total of 130 missions without aborts, the record for 8th Air Force Liberators.

Above.
During the summer of 1944, these B-24s of the 467th BG are dropping their loads over occupied France.
(USAAF)

The 790th Bomb Squadron insignia.

Typical Nissen hut accommodation at Rackheath airbase in Norfolk.

A gunner is pictured at his waist gun position. The B-24 belongs to the 789th BS.
(USAAF)

Bombs are exploding close to a nearly wrecked bridge.
(USAAF)

Right.
Back from a mission, sergeant Gillette examines the damage
caused by a Flak fragment, which shattered the armored glass
of his tail turret.
(USAAF)

Below and opposite page, bottom.
The B-24L 'School Daze' on the flight line at Rackheath base.
Its fuselage is left unpainted to save on weight and production
time. This is typical of 1945. A mechanic is touching up
the original nose art, which was partly hidden by additional
armor-plating.
(USAAF)

Above.
467th BG ships are pictured during a training flight near the English coast.
(USAAF)

A relaxed shot inside a B-24 cockpit. Note the 'Luckies' near the throttle levers.

In front of 'Tender Comrade,' whose shapely body is partly hidden by additional armor plate against Flak, colonel Albert Shower (the 467th BG CO) is congratulating lieutenant John Seward's crew of the 791st BS. They were the first crew of the group to complete its operational tour. This photo was taken on June 25, 1944 just after a mission over Pont-à-Vendin to support the Allied bridgehead in Normandy. Crewmembers are wearing F-2 electrical suits. A variety of flying gear is apparent: A-11, A-9 and B-6 helmets, B-3 and B-4 life jackets, B-8 and quick attachable chest (QAC) AN-6513-1A parachutes.
(USAAF)

Lieutenant J.J. Kish has pinned his Bombardier wings over a blue felt oblong (the 'Combat Flying Duty Patch') meaning he's assigned to a fighting unit. This was frequently displayed within AF units operating from England.
(USAAF)

Above.
B-24J 'Monster' (serial # 44-40166) of the 788th BS. This former 492nd BG machine was delivered to the 467th in August 1944. It flew combat missions with this squadron until war's end.

left.
**A damaged B-24 nose turret.
All the upper transparent
fairing has been torn off.**
(USAAF)

Right.
**A GMC refuelling truck parked
near a shark-nosed B-24 of the
467th BG. Regulation markings
on the fender indicate
that the vehicle is assigned
to the 8th Air Force,
789th Bomb Squadron,
467th Bomb. Group.**
(USAAF)

**Captain Horn, a photo officer
with the 467th BG, holds
a Kodak K-20 camera. Many cameras
like this one were carried to appraise
bomb patterns as soon as possible after
landing. Captain Horn is fitted with a B-3
jacket and non-modified A-6 flying
boots.**
(USAAF)

Below.
**Lieutenant T.H. Willis of the 467th BG is
pictured in his service uniform with
pilot wings and awards. The two first
ribbons are the Distinguished Flying
Cross and the Air Medal with an Oak
Leaf Cluster (OLC) for an additional
award.**
(USAAF)

Lieutenant Jenkins is pictured at the photo studio of the 467th BG base. His flight gear is composed of an A-11 flying helmet, AN-6530 goggles, A-14 oxygen mask fitted with an ANB-MC1 microphone. The leather jacket is the ubiquitous A-2 with painted-on rank bars on the shoulder loops. *(USAAF)*

Below.
On this October 14, 1944 photo, aircraft mechanics are photographed in front of a German propeller, which was probably shipped back to England for tests. The men are wearing herringbone twill (HBT) suits and A-3 mechanics' caps. Far right, an enlisted man has the shearling AN-J-4 jacket, an item of clothing normally reserved to aircrews. *(USAAF)*

This novelty bill was printed in England to celebrate the 200th mission of the 467th BG. One side shows the group insignia as well as its squadrons', and the symbols of the attached service units. The other side is partially dedicated to the most famous plane of the group: the 'Witchcraft,' and the four battle honors credited to the 467th. *(USAAF)*

B-24H 'Witchcraft'
(serial # 42-52534)
467th BG/790th BS -
October 1944. This plane flew
131 missions.
(Computer graphics by Nicolas Gohin)

Bottom.
Crew members of the 'Witchcraft' (790th BS/467th BG) are proudly posing in front of their
plane. This B-24 broke the record of 131 missions completed by the same plane over
Europe without aborts, and thus the heavier weight of bombs. It was displayed under
the Eiffel Tower in Paris with other famous planes of the 8th Air Force at the end of
the war. The mechanics have D-1 shearling jackets and A-3 herringbone twill caps.
The aircrew are wearing the F-2 electrically-heated suit, or the B-10 flying jacket with A-9
flying trousers donned over the F-3 electrically-heated suit.
(USAAF)

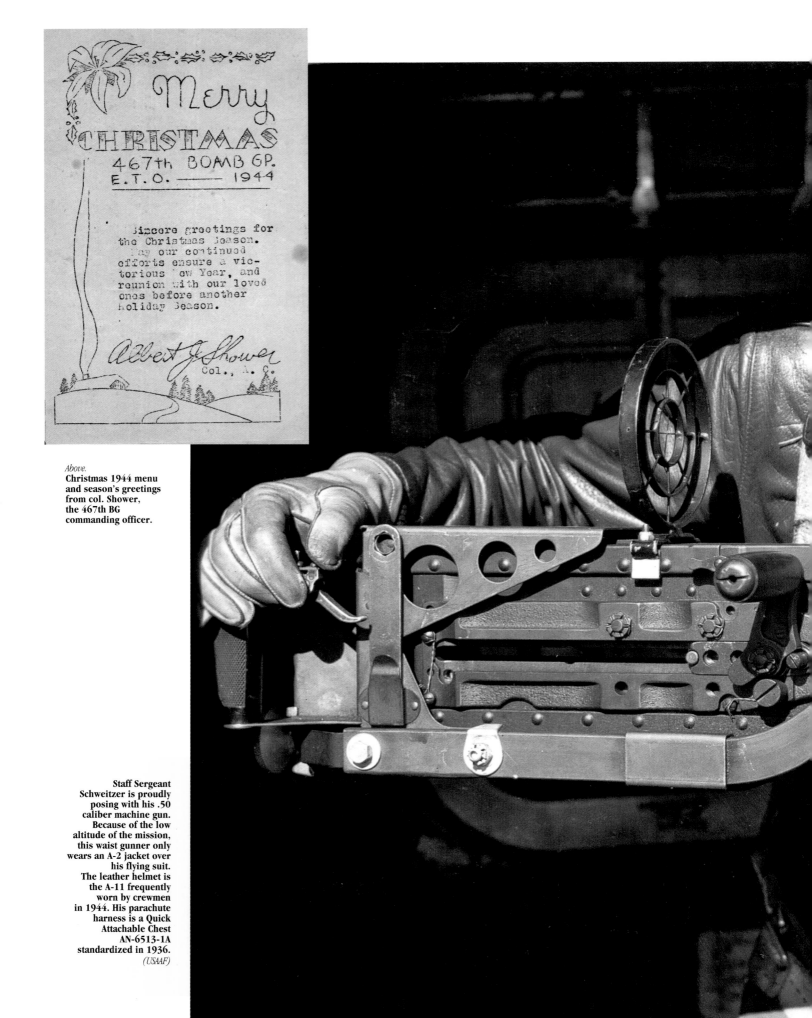

TO THE MEMORY OF FOUR GALLANT AMERICAN
AIRMEN OF THE 8TH AIR FORCE
2ND LT WILLIAM M. SHERRILL, TENNESSEE. T/SGT DARLTON W. PONTIUS, KANSAS
T/SGT GEORGE LIFSCHITZ, NEW YORK. S/SGT PHILIP A. SNYDER, PENNSYLVANIA
WHO LOST THEIR LIVES WHEN A LIBERATOR BOMBER RETURNING
FROM A RAID ON GERMANY CRASHED NEAR THIS CHURCH ON
THE 18TH AUGUST 1944. THIS MEMORIAL WAS PLACED HERE
BY THE PARISHIONERS OF KIRBY BEDON.

"LET US HAVE FAITH THAT RIGHT MAKES MIGHT
AND IN THAT FAITH LET US, TO THE END, DARE
TO DO OUR DUTY." ABRAHAM LINCOLN.

Left and above left.
**A plaque was
unveiled in a church
near Rackheath
airbase, to
commemorate the
crew of a B-24 that
crashed nearby
after a mission over
Germany.**
(USAAF)

**'Wolves Inc.' was flown
by the 791st BS (467th BG)
between May 1944 and
March 1945. It was lost
in the North Sea with
lieutenant Mills' crew as they
were on the way back from a
mission over Stuttgart:
there were only two survivors.**
(USAAF)

B-24J 'Wolves Inc.'
(serial # 41-28981) 467th
BG/791st BS - August 1944.
(Computer graphics by Nicolas Gohin)

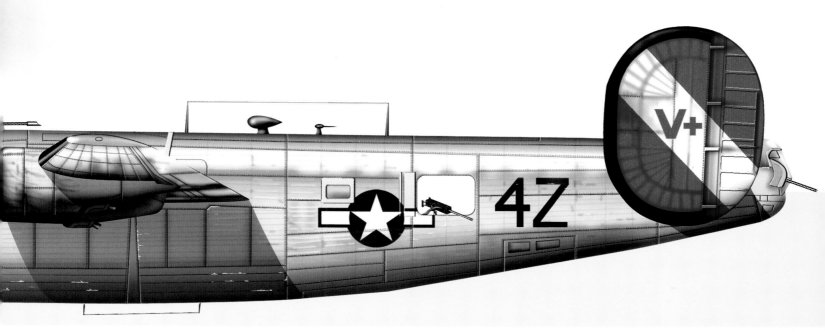

Right.
**An Air Medal awarding ceremony. These NCOs have been
ordered to fall in with the steel helmet, gas mask, and pistol
in the leather shoulder holster.**
(USAAF)

**This B-24 Liberator made a
twisted landing, ending its
course in the grass shoulder
of the runway, bending
the starboard landing gear.**
(USAAF)

The B-10 Flying jacket and its manufacturers tag

1. Sergeant Lee Malus' photo album. Malus hailed from New Orleans, he was a B-24 gunner with the 790th Bomb Squadron.
2. Guide to the Sioux Falls, South Dakota, AAF separation center, serving the stateside 2nd Air Force.
3. Season's greetings cards mailed by Malus to his mother.
4. An illustrated pamphlet about American Red Cross activities in Britain, also mailed by Malus on Jan. 4, 1945.
5. Pin-up girl postcard.
6. Poscard with the 790th Bomb Squadron insignia.
7. B-6 leather flying helmet.
8. A-10A oxygen mask, with the ANB-MC-1 microphone.
9. B-8 goggles.
10. Rayon scarf with USAAF logo.
11. Army issue 8th AF shoulder sleeve insignia.
12. A Guide on British culture for American servicemen.
13. A silver ring given by Consolidated Aircraft, the B-24 designer, and one of several manufacturers.
14. Silver ring decorated with the 8th AF insignia.

Above and previous page, top.
Back-type B-8 parachute.

Manufacturer's tag on the flying suit.

B-24 Pilot - June 1944

June 6, 1944 at Rackheath airbase. 467th BG crews are boarding their B-24s. The unit will raid bridges and coastal strongpoints in the Cherbourg sector, in support of the Normandy invasion.
This pilot is wearing light clothing for a short flight. Over the issue shirt and trousers, he has the following:
- Officer's service cap
- B-10 flying jacket
- B-4 life vest
- AN-S-31a summer flying suit
- issue leather service shoes
- B-8 back-type parachute.
Additional miscellaneous flying gear is carried in an M-1936 field bag and an aviator's kit bag.
Even if fighter opposition over the beachhead is nil, Flak will still be heavy. As protection against fragments, the pilot has an M-4 flak helmet, that will be donned over the target area, together with the flak jacket stowed inside the ship. Inside the helmet, used as a bag, can be seen our man's AN-6530 goggles and A-11 leather flying helmet.
(Reconstruction, photo Militaria Magazine)

167

CONFIDENTIAL   TARGET Victory   SEPT. 16, 1944   3

LET'S BRING 'EM BACK SAFE

If Hydraulic System
has gone out__

"No THANKS--
...no parachute
landing brakes...

TAKE ME TO WOODBRIDGE A/F "

WOODBRIDGE
RUNWAY

DO NOT TRY PARACHUTES FOR BRAKES

Above, left.
'Target Victory' was a
weekly bulleting
published by the 2nd Bombardment
Division HQ. It was printed "by and for combat flying personnel."
Classified as 'confidential,' it couldn't be taken outside
of the United Kingdom or during missions.

B-24s of the 467th BG are pictured during a mission. Sergeant Malus was a
gunner on the ship indicated by a cross.
(USAAF)

Above.
Page 3 of the 'Target Victory' issue of September 16, 1944.
If the hydraulic system had gone out, the use of parachutes as landing brakes was
frowned upon. The plane could try its luck at the Woodbridge emergency airfield,
which had a twice longer runway including a rise for added gravity braking and
grassed areas at both ends.

Below.
May 2, 1945, a 467th BG navigator lieutenant is being awarded the
Distinguished Flying Cross by colonel Albert J. Shower. The British-made 8th
AF shoulder patch and the 'Combat Flying Duty' patch are visible on the latter's
jacket. Both are wearing officer's collar insignia both on the shirt and blouse,
against regulations.
(USAAF)

Pages 4 and 5. As German jet fighters could be encountered more
frequently, it became urgent to advise gunners on updated aiming
techniques.
Being drawn from visual spottings, these silhouettes were still
tentative, but they could assist in fast identification. While the Me.262
and Me.163 were the more common types, the He.280 was still
in the test stage.
(USAAF)

SEPT. 16, 1944   TARGET Victory   CONFIDENTIAL   5

FINAL BRAINSTORM

ROCKET AND JET-FIGHTERS

HE. 280, JET.

ME. 163, ROCKET

LESS LIKELY TO MEET THESE

4   CONFIDENTIAL   TARGET Victory   SEPT. 16, 19

WARM YOUR GUNS FOR JERRY'S

You'll likely be meeting these soon and
our tip is you'd better sight 'em fir

ME. 262, JET.

POSITION FIRING

Angle Off	Rule For Present Fighters	Rule For ME163 and 262	Shake
90°	3 rads	2 1/2 rads	Reduce 1/2 rad
45°	2 rads	1 1/2 rads	Reduce 1/2 rad
22-1/2°	1 rad	1 rad	None
11-1/4°	1/2 rad	1/2 rad	None
0°	Point Blank	Point Blank	None

AIMING CHANGES LITTLE

12. 385TH BOMB. GROUP

548TH BOMB SQUADRON
LT. LUTHER WALLACE
PILOT

Above.
In March 1944, Wallace was pictured at Alexandria airbase in Louisiana before leaving for overseas. Wallace is kneeling, 2nd from left. Back row, from left to right: T/Sgt. Underwood, T/Sgt. McEachran, S/Sgt. Green, S/Sgt. Ramsey, S/Sgt. Josephson and S/Sgt Ross. Kneeling, from left to right are lieutenants Followell (plane commander), Wallace, Breckenridge and Yarema (bombardier). Upon Wallace's one before last flight, over Brest on Sept. 4, 1944, Yarema was struck by a flak shell fragment and died on the return flight. (USAAF)

The 385th Bomb Group insignia.

A portrait of Luther Wallace at flying school. He has a summer helmet with voice tubes instead of radio earphones, used in primary flight instruction for instructor-to-pupil communication.

The 548th Bomb Squadron insignia.

July 10
Tuesday

Dearest Mother and All,

There is not too much to write about, but must keep up my end of
the bargin. I rather like your new system of writing, getting a letter
every day or everyotherday is really good for the old morale. received
Mother's letter today dated the 30th. The rest have been coming in
about the same length of time. Don't worry about saying the something
over twice asit always sounds good. Received the clippings of me and
the one of Dan. I knew about Dan about a week after it happened, but
for the same reasonthat you didn't write about it, I didn't either I
went over to his Groupe about a week ago and talked to his C. O. and
The Intelligence Officer. At the time I was there, the report hewas
a P.W. had not come in. I was on this same raid and his group went
into the target afer us. His plane lost an engine over the target
dueto flak and left the formation with some P-38s escorting it home.
That was the last/they were seen. Evidently they lost another ####
engine, because if they had three engines they could Have made it O.K.
BECAUSE WE HAVE come home on three engines twice. Am going over again
to find out how to write to him, so if Mrs. McLaughlin doesn't know how
to write him let me know. I am still in the best of health and feeling
no pain. While I think about it, Have forgot to tell you about my dog
for the last month. My second time in London, was walking past a Pet
Shop and saw this brown Cocker-Spaniel in the window. I go in and
start petting him before I knew I was on the train back to the base with
a dow. He is really a good looking dog and I have his Pedigree for four
or five generations back. He was born Christmas Eve and is as big as
he will ever get now. Last night I was up most of the night with him.
He was quiet sick so today I took him to a veturrian Verernain, well anyway
a dog doctor. He gave me a bottle of medicen to give him so I guess he
will be O. K. He seems to like his new home because he has so many
to pet him around the squadron. Have plans to bring him home withme
when I come. Optomistic as Hell, ain't I. By the way I have sent my
Air Medal home, so be on the look out for it. One of the fellows here in
the barracks has finished his missions and has gone home. So I gave him
the medal to mail in the states. Come to think of it, I think I've already

A letter dated July 10, 1944 sent by Wallace to his
parents. He explains that he had been informed that
one of his friends had been shot down and captured
during a raid he had also taken part in. His friend's
ship lost an engine to Flak damage over the target and
left the formation with P-38s fighters escorting her. It
was the last time they were seen, they must have lost
another engine, because with three they could have
limped back to England.
Typewritten mail was probably hand-written mail that
had been censored.

Lieutenant Wallace was
pictured in a photo studio
before leaving
for overseas duty.
His dark olive drab
service coat has the
generic USAAF shoulder
patch, lieutenant 'butter
bars' on the shoulder
loops as well as
the Southeast Air Force
Training Center
distinctive insignia.
(DR)

Lieutenant Wallace's sterling silver pilot wings, made by Amico. These wings are worn by Wallace
on the adjoining picture.

Dearest Mother and all,

No doubt if I wee home you wuold like to spenk me for not writting. Has
been quiet some time since I wrote. I have just retrned form seven days at the
rest home. I have flown the last four missions as first pilot. Russ, Our pilot,
has been grounded for a few days so I took over the crew for a while. On my
twenty-ninth mission, we had a little bad luck over the target and it was only
the Lord himself that brought us back to the base. Yarema, our bombidier, the
short fellow in the picture got hit by a piece of flak and died on the way home.
The whole crew was pretty well shaken up so they sent us to the Rest Home for a
week. We went up to Scotland. A big beautifull house way out from everything.
We really did have a nice rest, enjoyed golf, tennia, horeseback riding and just
angthhng we wanted to do. Spent two days in Edingburg, Scotland which is a ver
old place. There are a few old castles there. We visted the one Mary, Queen of
Scots, lived. Really did see a lot of interesting sights. Most of all we got
a nice rest and are all set to go again. I have all the enlisted men from our
original crew and the rest of the officers are from another crew. As I said
I have 29 missions and am really sweating out the rest. Hope it won't be to
long. Had a pleasant surprise Saturday morning. Happer came up to see me. He

Extract of another letter sent by
Wallace to his parents in which
he tells that his plane was hit
by Flak during his 29th mission,
severely wounding Yarema,
the bombardier, who died
on the way back to England.

170

French Shower Gifts On Two Atlanta Fliers

Toccoa Second Looey, Over Six Months, Wins Captain's Bars, DFC, Presidential Citation

By MARGARET PEAVY

Two Atlantians a while back were dropping bombs on France and, every time they flew over, they were greeted by flak and fighter planes.... Now, that's all changed, report Lieutenant Claire L. Hutchinson (1018 Albion Avenue,) and Staff Sergeant Harold N. Carter (1113 Moreland Avenue, S. E.).... Instead of flak, they're greeted by friendly screams and yells and a profusion of gifts. ... Their outfit has been labeled "Brogger's Grocery Run" because now all they carry to France is food.... So it goes in war. ...

Here are some more lads whose love of aviation and freedom from fear of the open skies have served to make them valued nephews of Uncle Sam. ...

Technical Sergeant William H. Carroll, Vanderbilt graduate, of 612 Hardendorf Avenue, N. E., is an Air Medal recipient. ... Also wearing this medal is Sergeant Roy T. Hobby (565 Clifton Road, N. E.). ... Second Lieutenant

Robert A. Blackwood with the Air Transport Command in China won his Air Medal for operational flights over the "hump" of the mountains of Northern Burma. ... He's written his wife, the former Virginia Kirkland (106 Peachtree Battle Avenue), that his group has been cited by both President Roosevelt and Chiang Kaishek.... From Italy comes news of the same award going to First Lieutenant Eugene S. Love, of Atlanta. ...

A Troop Carrier Command in the European theater of operations has sent in a dispatch on First Lieutenant Thomas H. Ellison, of Atlanta ... "Tom" pilots a C-47, the only aircraft of its type performing at night in close formation, unarmed, unarmored, and yet flying in actual combat ... Tom flew one of the ships which dropped paratroopers on D-Day ... He's now won the Air Medal with two clusters ...

And the A. A. F. reports the air medal award has gone to Sergeant Joe C. Power, of 2534 Brookwood Drive and Sergeant Amon L. Knight, of McDonough, Ga.

Captain Ed McBrayer, of Toccoa, Ga., has a record to be proud of ... He went overseas six months ago as a second looey, and is now sporting captain's bars along with the Air Medal, Distinguished Flying Cross, and a Presidential citation ... His son, "Butch," was the recent recipient of "booties" made on the Isle of Capri, where his airman daddy lately was on a rest leave ...

Boys' high graduate, Luther R. Wallace (1057 Euclid Avenue, N. E.) has been decorated SIX times. A B-17 copilot, he wears the Distinguished Flying Cross in addition to the Air Medal and four clusters ...

Above.
Atlanta press article about lieutenant Wallace's operations in Europe, mentioning his award of the DFC and Air Medal with 4 oak leaf clusters.

Right.
6 August 1944. Lt. Wallace is pictured under the nose of 'Reluctant Lady.' He flew ten missions as co-pilot or pilot on this ship. Wallace is wearing a B-4 life jacket over an A-2 flying jacket, an A-3 parachute harness and a pair of earphones over his overseas cap.
(USAAF)

B-17G 'Reluctant Lady' (serial # 42-107035) 385th BG/548th BS - July 1944. Lt. Wallace flew ten missions in this plane.
(Computer graphics by Nicolas Gobin)

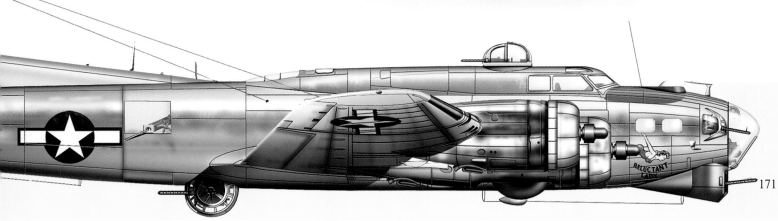

Right.
Close up of the F-3 heated suit, showing the connections between the jacket and trousers, and the gloves and jacket.

ENGLAND, OCTOBER 1944 385TH BOMB. GROUP B-17 GUNNER

Below.
The heated jacket manufacturer's label.

In the Great Ashfield base dressing room, this crewman has started by donning the F-3 heated suit. Reverting to electrically-heated liners, the USAAF adopted the F-3 at the beginning of 1944. The complete suit comprises:
- a pair of trouser liners with a lead and plug connected to a rheostat inside the plane
- a jacket liner with a short lead for connecting the trousers
- a pair a heated gloves plugged in thanks to a tab with snaps and a pair of felt booties, similar to those of the F-2 suit (see page 48). The latter were plugged in through tabs at the ankle. The suit is in lined nylon with an electrical wire sandwiched in between, in wide curves to cover the whole body. All heated gear being organizational equipment was usually stored in the clothing room, together with parachutes. These suits were turned in after each flight, and the supply room personnel ensured their drying and maintenance.

(Reconstruction, photo Militaria Magazine)

The electrically-heated trousers

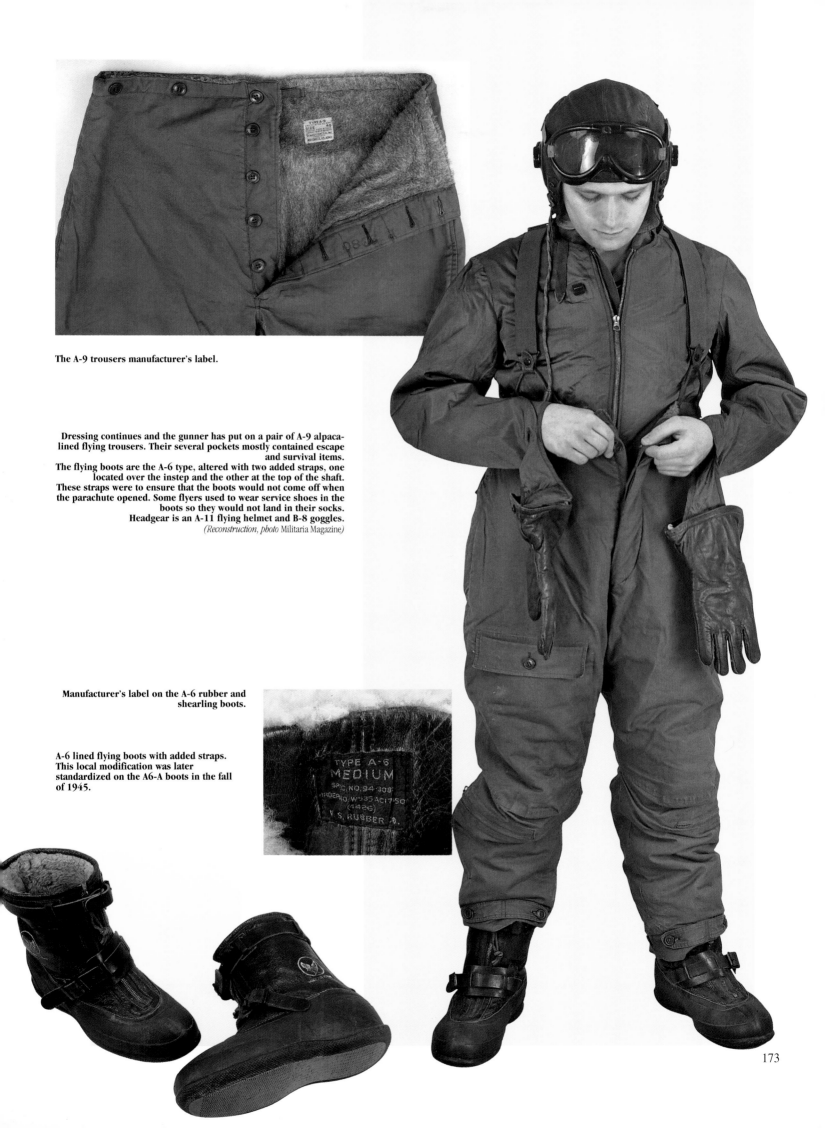

The A-9 trousers manufacturer's label.

Dressing continues and the gunner has put on a pair of A-9 alpaca-lined flying trousers. Their several pockets mostly contained escape and survival items.
The flying boots are the A-6 type, altered with two added straps, one located over the instep and the other at the top of the shaft. These straps were to ensure that the boots would not come off when the parachute opened. Some flyers used to wear service shoes in the boots so they would not land in their socks.
Headgear is an A-11 flying helmet and B-8 goggles.

(Reconstruction, photo Militaria Magazine*)*

Manufacturer's label on the A-6 rubber and shearling boots.

A-6 lined flying boots with added straps. This local modification was later standardized on the A6-A boots in the fall of 1945.

173

After donning a B-10 flying jacket, a B-4 type life vest and an A-3 parachute harness, our gunner is ready to board his ship. He holds the parachute chest pack in his left hand, the pack being stowed inside the plane before use.

The oxygen mask has an integral ANB-MC-1 microphone. All along the assembly phase, when all bomber formations gather to form the 'stream' towards the target, the electrically-heated suit remained unplugged. The main power lead hangs from a trouser pocket, within reach.
(Reconstruction, photo Militaria Magazine)

Parachute harness type A-3. Contrary to the AN-6513-1A, the hooks are located on the harness straps and not on the attachable chest pack. The elevators holding the hooks are sewn down on the harness front with a few breakable stitches. These would rip when the canopy opened, and the whole chest pack would fleet past the aviators' face, sometimes resulting in slight injuries.

Type A-3 parachute chest pack. The yellow marking indicates the chest packs that were compatible with A-3 harnesses. Packs which were used with the AN-6513-1A harness were identified by a red marking.

8th Air Force British-made shoulder patch, in distinctive yellow (instead of orange) embroidery on blue felt, worn by lieutenant Wallace on his wool service coat.

Below, right.
This wire was sent by lieutenant Wallace to his parents informing them that he had completed his mission tour.

Bottom right.
Two of Wallace's decorations: on the right his Air Medal, on the left the Distinguished Flying Cross (DFC). Wallace had mailed his medals to his mother as he had just been awarded them, the reason why there are no Oak leaf clusters on the Air Medal ribbon.

Back home, lieutenant Wallace was photographed in uniform in an attractive convertible.
(RR)

MISSIONS LOG
LT. LUTHER WALLACE (385TH BOMB GROUP/548TH BOMB SQUADRON)

Upon leaving the USA (Alexandria Air Base in Louisiana), Lt. Wallace was co-pilot on Lt. Followell's crew as follows:

Wallace mission #	385th BG mission #	Date	Target	B-17 serial No	B-17 name	Remarks
1	111	22 May 1944	Kiel	42-97307	None	
2	115	27 May 1944	Karlsruhe	42-3490	None	
3	117	29 May 1944	Leipzig	42-102486	None	
4	118	30 May 1944	Hamm	42-31833	Mickey II	
5	119	31 May 1944	Hamm	42-107035	Reluctant Lady	
6	120	02 June 1944	Equihen	42-107035	Reluctant Lady	
7	125	05 June 1944	Benvoir	42-97079	Dozy Doats	Wallace flew as co-pilot on the Wells crew, this mission only
8	126	06 June 1944	Caen	43-37548	None	
9	128 *	06 June 1944	Argentan	43-37548	None	
10	130	08 June 1944	Nantes	42-107035	Reluctant Lady	
11	131	11 June 1944	Le Touquet	?	?	Wallace didn't fly this date
12	132	12 June 1944	Montdidier	?	?	Wallace didn't fly this date
13	133	14 June 1944	Florennes	42-107035	Reluctant Lady	
14	135	18 June 1944	Hannover	42-107035	Reluctant Lady	
15	137	20 June 1944	Fallerseiben	42-107035	Reluctant Lady	
16	140	23 June 1944	Edernay	42-107035	Reluctant Lady	
17	142	25 June 1944	Marquee Drop	42-107035	Reluctant Lady	
18	159	28 June 1944	Merseburg	42-102486	None	
19	160	29 June 1944	Merseburg	42-107035	Reluctant Lady	
20	161	30 June 1944	Munich	42-102481	Kentucky Winner	
21	162	01 August 1944	Marquee Drop	42-31833	Mickey II	

For the next 6 missions Wallace had his own crew as follows:

22	168	08 August 1944	Ground support	42-97079	Dozy Doats	
23	175	18 August 1944	St. Dizier	43-38060	Texas Bluebonnet	
24	176	24 August 1944	Brux	42-107035	Reluctant Lady	
25	177	25 August 1944	Rechlin	42-38035	Mr. Lucky	
26	178	26 August 1944	Brest	43-38060	Texas Bluebonnet	
27	179	27 August 1944	Berlin	42-97079	Dozy Doats	

For the next 2 missions Wallace was co-pilot with Followell's crew again

28	181	03 Sept. 1944	Brest	42-98016	None	
29	182	05 Sept. 1944	Brest	42-102679	Mississippi Miss	

13. 351ST BOMB. GROUP

ANONYMOUS PHOTO ALBUM

Established on September 25, 1942, the 351st Bomb. Group consisted of 4 squadrons (508, 509, 510 and 511th BS). It moved to England between April and May 1943 under colonel William A. Hatcher and was based at Polebrook (Station # 110). Operations began in May 1943 with the overall strategic campaign against occupied Europe. The 351st received a first Distinctive Unit Citation for the accurate bombardment of an aircraft factory in central Germany, in spite of heavy Flak and pressing enemy fighters, and a second one for its part in the successful attack on January 11, 1944 of more aircraft factories in the same area. Between February 20 and 25, 1944 the 351st BG was involved in the 'Big Week.' Two of its members were posthumously awarded the Medal of Honor: Lt. Walter E. Truemper (navigator) and sergeant Archibald Mathies (engineer). Their aircraft badly damaged by a direct Flak hit, the co-pilot dead and pilot severely injured, Truemper and Mathies managed to fly the plane until other crewmembers could bail out. In an effort to save the pilot on the third attempt to land in England, the bomber crashed. The 351st BG bombed strongpoints on the coast on D-Day and supported ground troops for the Saint-Lô breakout in July. In September, the group hit enemy positions to cover operation Market Garden in The Netherlands. During the Battle of the Bulge, the 351st struck front-line positions and airfields to hinder the German counteroffensive. The unit then flew several missions to support airborne troops during operation Varsity (the crossing of the Rhine). Just after V-E Day, the 351st returned to the USA where it was inactivated on August 28, 1945. Between May 1943 and April 1945, the 351st BG lost 124 bombers in action.

The 351st Bomb. Group insignia

Title.
A brand new B-17G of the 351st BG during a mission. No nose art has been painted yet.
(USAAF)

Right.
These two members of the photo section are debating about adding a new picture to the large gallery which is already adorning the walls. Most of these are 'cheese' shots of actresses.
(USAAF)

Under the nose of 'Gremlin's Delight,' boasting 9 kills, three members of the 351st BG are posing for the photographer. From right to left: T/Sgt. Frany, Lts. Werth and Don. Note the painted group insignia and gunner wings on the NCO's A-2 jacket.
(USAAF)

Full throttle! This B-17G named 'Slow Ball' (serial # 42-97492) is about to take off from the Polebrook strip. The bombardier is already at his station in the nose.
(USAAF)

The B-17F 'My Devotion' (serial # 42-30857) had flown 31 missions when this picture was taken in the summer of 1943.
(USAAF)

Its hydraulics shot to pieces, a B-17G of the 508th BS is making a belly landing on the runway's grassy shoulder. The lower ball turret has been cranked up into the fuselage.
(USAAF)

Right.
June 11, 1943: armorers are about to lift a bomb inside the bomber's bay.
(USAAF)

'Snoozin' Susan' (serial # 42-29860) parked at the Polebrook airbase.
(USAAF)

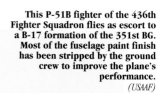

This P-51B fighter of the 436th
Fighter Squadron flies as escort to
a B-17 formation of the 351st BG.
Most of the fuselage paint finish
has been stripped by the ground
crew to improve the plane's
performance.
(USAAF)

Above.

**After a belly landing, ground crewmen of the 351st BG are
fussing around a B-17G.**
(USAAF)

This crew has safely achieved a belly landing at the Polebrook
base. Three crew members have pinned a whistle near
the jacket collar of their flight jacket, the man standing
second from left has an RAF parachute harness, with
the better quick-release box. Most of them are wearing
the A-4 flight suit modified with zippers on the outer pockets,
except the man on far right who has a pair of HBT fatigue
trousers.
(USAAF)

In the thick of things! This shot was taken from a waist gunner's station. The closest plane, 'Hubba Hubba!' (serial #43-37557), code YB-K, belonged to the 508th Bomb. Squadron. *(USAAF)*

Assigned to the 351st BG as Armament officer in 1943, Hollywood star Clark Gable (of 'Gone with the wind' fame) featured in many propaganda movies to stimulate Airforce enlistments. Clad in an elegant officer's regulation trench coat, captain Gable is pictured with another officer and three sergeants, probably gunners, near the tail MGs of a B-17. *(USAAF)*

Captain Gable with another officer in front of a Flying Fortress. Gable sports embroidered gunner wings on his British-style blouse. *(USAAF)*

Previous page.
Set on a navigation chart of Bremen are:
- B-6 flying helmet with earcups for the ANB-H1 earphones
- AN-6530 goggles
- Officer garrison cap with bullion lieutenant's bar
- Private purchase officer service cap by Bancroft
- Pilot's notes
- A-9 winter flying gloves
- A March 1943 London edition of the *Stars and Stripes* featuring 8th Airforce bomber operations on page One
- ANB-H1 earphones and headband
- A Guide to Great Britain for American servicemen
- London tube and city maps.

These gunners are checking the twin tail MGs of a B-17, while the gunner activates them from his station in the plane. *(USAAF)*

On 6 June 1943, Clark Gable is in flying gear (A-4 suit, B-6 leather helmet and B-7 goggles) at a waist gun position for a photo session. Note the electrical plug of his heated gloves, which probably are British modified gloves. Due to the lack of standard D-1 heated boots and C-1 gloves, RAF items were adapted for the F-1 electrically-heated undersuit.

Gable arrived in England in April 1943 with the task of making an educational film about bomber gunners. Before being assigned to the 351st BG, he decided to start shooting with the famous 303rd BG ('Hell's Angels'). He flew five actual combat missions and his ship was attacked four times by fighters. But it was unthinkable that he'd be captured by the Germans and exhibited like a circus animal, so he was quickly taken off combat status.

(USAAF)

The type B-2, Cap, flying winter. The earflap is raised on the sides.

The manufacturer's label indicates a 1942 contract.

TYPE B-2
SIZE 7¼
SPEC. NO.94-3098
A.C. ORD. NO.42-841-P
WERBER SPORTSWEAR CO
NEWBURGH, N.Y.

This B-17F of the 351st BG is taking off from Polebrook airbase with additional bombs under the wing roots. This increased load was possible for short range missions.
(USAAF)

NAVIGATOR AND BOMBARDIER, OCTOBER 1943

October 10, 1943: this navigator and bombardier are walking to their ship. In a few hours, their 'Fort' will fly over Munster in Germany. Enclosed in the plane nose, these officers' task will be to pinpoint the railtracks. For the moment, they are lugging various items of flying equipment in an issue Aviator's kit bag.

The navigator (left) holds the shell of a standard M1 steel helmet, which will fit over the sheepskin flying helmet. Heavier flying boots will replace the service shoes on board. The rest of his uniform is as follows:
- Officer cap
- A-2 leather flying jacket
- B-3 life preserver
- modified A-4 flying suit
- AN-6513-1a chest parachute harness
- A-8B oxygen mask
- a neck cloth fashioned out of parachute silk
- a pair of A-10 gloves, slipped behind a harness strap.

The navigator (right) carries instruments and charts in a leather case. He has a pair of sheepskin A-9 gloves. A metal whistle has been pinned by the collar of the A-2 jacket, he has donned an A-4 suit. The remaining of his gear is as follows:
- B-2 sheepskin cap
- ANB-H1 earphones and headband
- Unaltered A-6 heavy flying boots
- B-4 life preserver
- Back-type B-8 chute.

(Reconstruction, photo by Militaria Magazine)

Above.
Guided by smoke markers dropped by the Pathfinder planes, this B-17 with its bay open is about to complete its bomb run.
(USAAF)

This 508th BS lieutenant (note the squadron patch on his jacket) is pointing at the slogan painted by a waist gunner below his firing position. Also note the kill sign.
(USAAF)

The arrival of the P-51 Mustang fighter in the European theater of operations in November 1943 was a major event. Fitted with auxiliary tanks, the P-51 could escort the bombers all the way into Germany and back, and proved a worthy opponent to the Fw.190. Its massive commitment was another weakening factor for the Luftwaffe who, confronted with large numbers of these aggressive aircraft, had to fight them before attempting to reach the heavy bombers. This P-51B of the 354th Fighter Group (the first to receive the Mustang) was photographed during a visit at the Polebrook base on December 27, 1943.
(USAAF)

Waiting for the completion of the gasoline refuelling, the crew of 'Stormy weather' are sorting out their flying gear.
(USAAF)

After the landing, medical personnel are evacuating a wounded gunner. Note the lack of unit sign on the tail of the plane, indicating that this photo was taken during the first missions of the 351st BG.
(USAAF)

These are the 11 crew members of the 'Gremlin Castle' and their crew chief (far right). Note the strange headgear of the 2nd man standing from the right. The visor and earcups suggest a hand-made hybrid obtained from a B-2 cap and a B-6 flying helmet. Most of the chest pack parachute harnesses are British-issue.
(USAAF)

Above.
The Nose Art of 'Rockaway Babe II' seems to fascinate these mechanics. Note the aluminum fairing that covers the chin turret well.
(USAAF)

14. 25TH BOMB GROUP

362D WEATHER RECONNAISSANCE SQUADRON TECHNICAL SERGEANT JAMES T. RYON, AIRPLANE MECHANIC

Despite of its original function and title, the 25th Bomb. Group was a reconnaissance unit assigned to the 325th Photo Weather Reconnaissance (PWR) Wing. The unit became the actual 'eyes of the 8th Air Force.' It was activated on Easter 1944 at Station 376 (Watton) in England. The group consisted of three squadrons, the 652nd Bomb Squadron (Heavy), 653rd Bomb Squadron (Light) and the 654th Bomb Squadron (Special).

The 652nd squadron flew mainly B-17 Gs, but also the B–24 D and H. Its missions were long range weather flights over the Atlantic (code-named 'Epicure'). Weather readings were taken every 50 miles at altitudes varying from 50 to 30,000 feet, the average flight time being over 12 hours. For thirteen months, the 652nd Squadron maintained an average of 1.5 to 2 aircraft in the air over the Atlantic at all hours of the day and night.

The 653rd and the 654th squadrons flew British two-engined De Haviland Mosquitoes. They flew completely unarmed, relying on their speed and altitude to keep out of trouble.

Planes flew singly with a pilot and navigator, the latter trained in meteorology. These men were often veteran bomber crews with a tour of operations under their belts. Most of these missions were night photography flights code-named 'Joker.'

The 652nd Bomb Squadron insignia.

GUARD WITH POWER

The 25th Bomb Group insignia.

T/Sgt James Ryon pictured in England while on a pass.
(USAAF)

When there was no moon, the navigator had to rely on his skills and the 'Gee' beacon to locate the target in the dark. The light source was created by M-46 photoflash bombs, twelve being loaded in the bomb bay.

This certificate was awarded to T/Sgt. Ryon for meritorious service while assigned to the 652nd Bomb Squadron between February 10, 1944 and May 8, 1945.

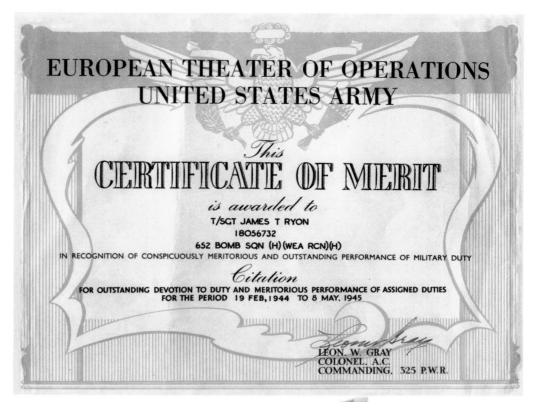

EUROPEAN THEATER OF OPERATIONS
UNITED STATES ARMY

This

CERTIFICATE OF MERIT

is awarded to

T/SGT JAMES T RYON
18056732
652 BOMB SQN (H)(WEA RCN)(H)

IN RECOGNITION OF CONSPICUOUSLY MERITORIOUS AND OUTSTANDING PERFORMANCE OF MILITARY DUTY

Citation

FOR OUTSTANDING DEVOTION TO DUTY AND MERITORIOUS PERFORMANCE OF ASSIGNED DUTIES
FOR THE PERIOD 19 FEB, 1944 TO 8 MAY, 1945

LEON. W. GRAY
COLONEL, A.C.
COMMANDING, 325 P.W.R.

On Watton airbase, a 25th Bomb Group Mosquito is ready to take off on a photo mission. *(RR)*

Below.
These three mechanics are pictured under the nose of a B-17 of the 652nd BS, whose insignia can be clearly seen.
(USAAF)

Crew Chief on a B-17 Flying Fortress, T|Sgt. James T. Ryon of An Eighth Air Force Reconnaissance Station, England. As the Gorman is one of the skilled technicians who make it possible for Eighth Air Force planes to continue their around the clock missions over Germany. He has charge of the mechanics who service and repair this craft, that flies in support of Eighth Air Force bombing raids.

B-17's and Mosquitos from here make lone missions over Europe and the North Atlantic, gathering weather data for future air and ground operations against the enemy. Mosquitos are used as photographic and reconnaissance planes as well, filming German installations by day and night to scout the way for Eighth Air Force heavies, then returning after raids to picture the damage done.

T|Sgt. Ryon, the son of Mr. J. E. Ryon of Gorman, is a graduate of Dublin High School. An oil field worker, he entered the army in August, 1941 and has been overseas since August, 1942, having been awarded the European Theater of Operations Ribbon with Bronze Star for participation of his unit in the aerial warfare over western Europe.

Above.
During the summer of 1944, these mechanics are pictured near a plane of the unit. Most are wearing the one-piece herringbone twill suit issued to ground crews for their work.

James Ryon's pals during a leave in London, probably on 'Rainbow corner' at Piccadilly.

This press article about Tech. Sgt Ryon and his unit in England was published in the USA.

This USAAF serviceman is getting on well with a WAAF (Royal Air Force woman auxiliary).

Right and below, right.
Two 25th BG 'Forts' and their maintenance teams. Note that defensive armament was taken down from most of the group's ships, such as 'Eli's son.'
(USAAF)

Below.
Sergeant Ryon servicing a B-17G power plant in the summer of 1944.
(USAAF)

'Lilly Ann,' a 652nd Bomb Squadron B-17G is totally devoid of armament. The former chin turret location is clearly visible.
(USAAF)

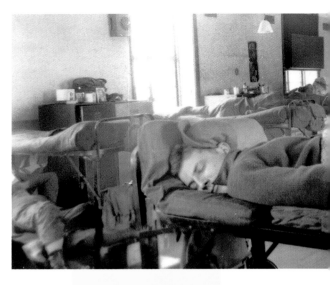

Exhausted by very hard work to keep the planes operational, this mechanic deserved some hours of good sleep.
(USAAF)

Left.
Major Podjowski, the 652d BS commanding officer, discussing with mechanics in front of a B-17.
(USAAF)

Below.
Watton airbase: this B-17 crew of the 652nd BS stops for a picture after a flight. Note the wearing of B-10 and A-2 flight jackets, as well as the type A-3 parachute harnesses and AN-S-31 flight suits.
(USAAF)

Mechanics are changing a tire on a B-17 main wheel. This home-made machine using a hydraulic jack had been devised to prevent injury in case of improper handling. *(USAAF)*

Left.
Garbed in their thick shearling garments, these ground crewmembers are attending a football game. *(DR)*

The mobile platforms for working on the engines are clearly visible. No less than eight men under a crew chief were required to service a single bomber.
(USAAF)

A factory-fresh B-24H of the 760th BS (467th BG) drops its twelve 500 pounders over the target area.

ACKNOWLEDGMENTS

This work would never have been possible but for the support and the assistance of several persons:
– I am especially indebted to William Varnedoe Jr., president of 385th BG Association, for his help, his availability and his kind authorization to use certain parts of his book *The Story of Van's Valiants in the 8th Air Force - The 385th Bomb Group, a New History*, Mrs. Marion Courtad for her kind authorization concerning her husband's photos and archives, Kim Larick for her assistance in gathering the personal archives of Sergeant Irvin Courtad, Bill Davenport Historian of the 446th BG Association, Lawrey Spencer, Harold Kiena,
– Philippe Charbonnier, editor of *Militaria Magazine,* for his trust and assistance,
– Frederic Finel, Christophe Deschodt, Remi Longetti, Mathieu Bianchi, Jean-Charles Postel, Luc Ristor, the militaria shop 'Overlord' at 96, rue de la Folie Mericourt 75011 Paris, for lending several pieces their collections for photographing,
– But also my parents, Barbara Catalano, Bruno Chapelle, David Warren (webmaster of www.447bg.com), Richard White, Vernon Shattuck, Philip Clark, Bruno Alberti, Jean-Michel Besson, Olivier Cantal, Laurent Bianchi, Guillaume Fisher, Olivier Cailloux, Philippe Ferbert and Romain Heuzey.

Gregory Pons

BIBLIOGRAPHY

– *The Story of Van's Valiants in the 8th Air Force - The 385th Bomb Group, a New History*, William W. Varnedoe Jr., McNally Productions 2003

– *History of the 385th Bombardment Group (Heavy)*, Lt. Colonel Marston S. Leonard USAF (Ret.), Newsfoto Publishing 1946

– *History of the 447th Bomb Group*, Doyle Shields 1996

– *Ridgewell's Flying Fortresses, the 381st Bombardment Group (H) in World War II*, Ron MacKay - Schiffer Publishing 2000

– *379th Bombardment Group Anthology* Vols. I and II, Turner Publishing Company 2000

– *381st Bomb. Group*, Ron MacKay, Squadron/Signal Publications 1994

– *The History of the 446th Bomb Group (H) 1943-1945*, Harold E. Jansen

– *Air Force Combat Units of World War II* - Department of the Air Force, Chartwell 1994

– *Liberator Album - B-24s of the 2nd Air Division USAAF*, Mike Bailey & Tony North, Midland Publishing Limited 1998

– *B-17 Flying Fortress Units of the Eighth Air Force (part 1 & 2)*, Martin Bowman, Osprey publishing 2000-2002

– *B-24 Liberator Units of the Eighth Air Force*, Robert F. Dorr, Osprey publishing 1999

– *Strangers in a strange land, Vol. II Escape to Neutrality*, Hans Heini & Gino Künzle, Squadron/Signal Publications 1992

– *The Mighty Eighth War Manual*, Roger A. Freeman, Cassel & Co 1984/2001

– *The Army Air Forces in World War II - vol. II & III*, W.F. Craven & J.L. Cate, University of Chicago Press 1949/1958

– *Target Berlin - Mission 250: 6 March 1944*, Jef. Ethell & Dr. A. Price, Greenhill books 1981

– *Last Hope, the Blood Chit Story*, R.E. Baldwin & Thomas Wm. McGarry, Schiffer Publishing 1997

– *The Mighty Eighth War Diary*, Roger A. Freeman, Alan Crouchman & Vic Maslen, Arms and Armour Press 1981

– *The Eighth Air Force in Camera 1942-1944*, Martin W. Bowman, Sutton publishing 1997

– *The Eighth Air Force in Camera 1944-1945*, Martin W. Bowman - Sutton publishing 1998

– *B-24 Nose Art Name Directory,* Wallace R. Forman, Specialty Press 1996

– *B-17 Nose Art Name Directory*, Wallace R. Forman, Phalanx 1996.

Translated from the French by Gregory PONS and Philippe CHARBONNIER — Design, and lay-out by Philippe CHARBONNIER and Magali MASSELIN

© *Histoire & Collections 2006*

ISBN: 2-915239-82-7
Publish number: 2-915239

© *Histoire & Collections 2006*

A book published by
HISTOIRE & COLLECTIONS
SA au capital de 182 938, 82 €
5, avenue de la République F-75541 Paris Cédex 11

▶ N°Indigo 0 820 888 911
0,118 € TTC / MN

Fax 01 47 00 51 11
www.histoireetcollections.fr

This book has been designed, typed, laid-out and processed by *Histoire & Collections*, and *Studio A&C* fully on integrated computer equipment

Printed by Zure
Spain, European Union
May 2006